current price £5.95.

JMSmith.
1963.

THE CAMBRIDGE BIBLE COMMENTARY

NEW ENGLISH BIBLE

General Editors: P. R. ACKROYD, A. R. C. LEANEY, J. W. PACKER

THE BOOKS OF
AMOS, HOSEA
AND MICAH

COMMENTARY BY

HENRY McKEATING

Lecturer in Theology, University of Nottingham

CAMBRIDGE
AT THE UNIVERSITY PRESS
1971

Published by the Syndics of the Cambridge University Press
Bentley House, 200 Euston Road, London NW1 2DB
American Branch: 32 East 57th Street, New York, N.Y.10022

© Cambridge University Press 1971

ISBNS:
0 521 08133 5 clothbound
0 521 09647 2 paperback

Printed in Great Britain
at the University Printing House, Cambridge
(Brooke Crutchley, University Printer)

GENERAL EDITORS' PREFACE

The aim of this series is to provide the text of the New English Bible closely linked to a commentary in which the results of modern scholarship are made available to the general reader. Teachers and young people have been especially kept in mind. The commentators have been asked to assume no specialized theological knowledge, and no knowledge of Greek and Hebrew. Bare references to other literature and multiple references to other parts of the Bible have been avoided. Actual quotations have been given as often as possible.

The completion of the New Testament part of the series in 1967 provides a basis upon which the production of the much larger Old Testament and Apocrypha series can be undertaken. The welcome accorded to the series has been an encouragement to the editors to follow the same general pattern, and an attempt has been made to take account of criticisms which have been offered. One necessary change is the inclusion of the translators' footnotes since in the Old Testament these are more extensive, and essential for the understanding of the text.

Within the severe limits imposed by the size and scope of the series, each commentator will attempt to set out the main findings of recent biblical scholarship and to describe the historical background to the text. The main theological issues will also be critically discussed.

Much attention has been given to the form of the volumes. The aim is to produce books each of which will be read consecutively from first to last page. The introductory material leads naturally into the text, which itself leads into the alternating sections of the commentary.

The series is accompanied by three volumes of a more general character. *Understanding the Old Testament* sets out to provide the larger historical and archaeological background, to say something about the life and thought of the people of the Old Testament, and to answer the question 'Why should we study the Old Testament?'. *The Making of the Old Testament* is concerned with the formation of the books of the Old Testament and Apocrypha in the context of the ancient near eastern world, and with the ways in which these books have come down to us in the life of the Jewish and Christian communities. *Old Testament Illustrations* contains maps, diagrams and photographs with an explanatory text. These three volumes are designed to provide material helpful to the understanding of the individual books and their commentaries, but they are also prepared so as to be of use quite independently.

P. R. A.
A. R. C. L.
J. W. P.

CONTENTS

LIST OF MAPS AND CHART

THE FOOTNOTES TO THE
N.E.B. TEXT

The footnotes to the N.E.B. text are designed to help the reader either to understand particular points of detail – the meaning of a name, the presence of a play upon words – or to give information about the actual text. Where the Hebrew text appears to be erroneous, or there is doubt about its precise meaning, it may be necessary to turn to manuscripts which offer a different wording, or to ancient translations of the text which may suggest a better reading, or to offer a new explanation based upon conjecture. In such cases, the footnotes supply very briefly an indication of the evidence, and whether the solution proposed is one that is regarded as possible or as probable. Various abbreviations are used in the footnotes:

(1) Some abbreviations are simply of terms used in explaining a point: *ch(s).*, chapter(s); *cp.*, compare; *lit.*, literally; *mng.*, meaning; *MS(S).*, manuscript(s), i.e. Hebrew manuscript(s), unless otherwise stated; *om.*, omit(s); *or*, indicating an alternative interpretation; *poss.*, possible; *prob.*, probable; *rdg.*, reading.

(2) Other abbreviations indicate sources of information from which better interpretations or readings may be obtained.

Aq. Aquila, a Greek translator of the Old Testament (perhaps about A.D. 130) characterized by great literalness.

Aram. Aramaic – may refer to the text in this language (used in parts of Ezra and Daniel), or to the meaning of an Aramaic word. Aramaic belongs to the same language family as Hebrew, and is known from about 1000 B.C. over a wide area of the Middle East, including Palestine.

Heb. Hebrew – may refer to the Hebrew text or may indicate the literal meaning of the Hebrew word.

Josephus Flavius Josephus (A.D. 37/8–about 100), author of the *Jewish Antiquities*, a survey of the whole history of his people, directed partly at least to a non-Jewish audience, and of various other works, notably one on the *Jewish War* (that of A.D. 66–73) and a defence of Judaism (*Against Apion*).

Luc. Sept. Lucian's recension of the Septuagint, an important edition made in Antioch in Syria about the end of the third century A.D.

Pesh.   Peshitta or Peshitto, the Syriac version of the Old Testament. Syriac is the name given chiefly to a form of Eastern Aramaic used by the Christian community. The translation varies in quality, and is at many points influenced by the Septuagint or the Targums.

Sam.   Samaritan Pentateuch – the form of the first five books of the Old Testament as used by the Samaritan community. It is written in Hebrew in a special form of the Old Hebrew script, and preserves an important form of the text, somewhat influenced by Samaritan ideas.

Scroll(s)   Scroll(s), commonly called the Dead Sea Scrolls, found at or near Qumran from 1947 onwards. These important manuscripts shed light on the state of the Hebrew text as it was developing in the last centuries B.C. and the first century A.D.

Sept.   Septuagint (meaning 'seventy'; often abbreviated as the Roman numeral LXX), the name given to the main Greek version of the Old Testament. According to tradition, the Pentateuch was translated in Egypt in the third century B.C. by 70 (or 72) translators, six from each tribe, but the precise nature of its origin and development is not fully known. It was intended to provide Greek-speaking Jews with a convenient translation. Subsequently it came to be much revered by the Christian community.

Symm.   Symmachus, another Greek translator of the Old Testament (beginning of the third century A.D.), who tried to combine literalness with good style. Both Lucian and Jerome viewed his version with favour.

Targ.   Targum, a name given to various Aramaic versions of the Old Testament, produced over a long period and eventually standardized, for the use of Aramaic-speaking Jews.

Theod.   Theodotion, the author of a revision of the Septuagint (probably second century A.D.), very dependent on the Hebrew text.

Vulg.   Vulgate, the most important Latin version of the Old Testament, produced by Jerome about A.D. 400, and the text most used throughout the Middle Ages in western Christianity.

[...]   In the text itself square brackets are used to indicate probably late additions to the Hebrew text.

(Fuller discussion of a number of these points may be found in *The Making of the Old Testament* in this series)

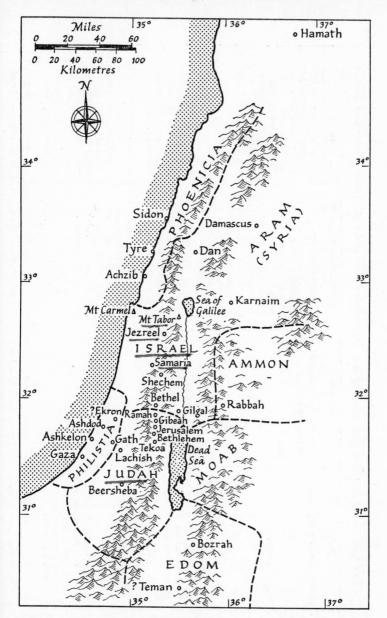

1. This map of eighth-century Palestine shows most of the places mentioned in Amos, Hosea and Micah. The only exceptions are foreign places which fall outside the area which the map covers, and one or two places whose locality is not sufficiently accurately known to allow them to be indicated.

Table of events in the eighth century B.C. bearing on the books of Amos, Hosea and Micah

Judah	Prophets	The Northern Kingdom	Assyria
Uzziah (Azariah) 783–742	Amos – at very end of reign of Jeroboam	Jeroboam II 786–746	Assyria weak for first half of century. A period of peace and prosperity for Israel and Judah
Jotham 742–735	Isaiah*	Zechariah 746–745. Murdered after six months' reign	Tiglath Pileser 745–727. Assyria gathered strength under his rule
		Shallum 745. Assassinated after one month	
		Menahem 745–738. Accepted Assyrian sovereignty and paid heavy tribute	
		Pekahiah 738–737. Assassinated	
	Hosea probably active through most of this period	Pekah 737–732. Reversed Menahem's foreign policy. Put himself at head of anti-Assyrian coalition and attacked Judah, who had refused to join	Assyria came to Judah's aid in 732. Overthrew the other members of the coalition (Syria and Philistia) and attacked Israel
Ahaz 735–715. When attacked by Pekah and his allies, appealed for Assyrian help		Hoshea 732–724. Murdered Pekah and surrendered to the Assyrians. But at the death of Shalmaneser rebelled again	Shalmaneser V 727–722
	Micah active for unspecified period before and after fall of Samaria	722/1 END OF NORTHERN KINGDOM	Sargon II 722–705. Destroyed Samaria in 722/1 and made Israel into an Assyrian province
Hezekiah 715–687. Rebelled against Assyria and forced by Sennacherib to pay tribute Manasseh 687–642. Accepted Assyrian domination			Sennacherib 705–681. Invaded Judah in 701, and probably again later

* Isaiah was active from the last year of Uzziah, and may have been still alive at the beginning of the reign of Manasseh.

x

THE BOOKS OF
AMOS, HOSEA AND MICAH

✳ ✳ ✳ ✳ ✳ ✳ ✳ ✳ ✳ ✳ ✳ ✳ ✳ ✳

ISRAEL AND JUDAH IN THE EIGHTH CENTURY

The eighth century falls fairly neatly into two contrasting halves. The first half was for both Israel and Judah a kind of Victorian age, a half-century of great stability and national prosperity, and covered by the reign of a single monarch, Uzziah (alias Azariah), in the south, and Jeroboam II in the north. Such periods for the Palestinian states could only occur when there was no great power strong enough to make life difficult for them; they were therefore rare. Egypt was not strong, and Assyria, which had been active towards the end of the previous century (around the end of the reign of Ahab and subsequently), was for the time being quiescent.

In one other way we may call this period a Victorian age. The national wealth was not at all equitably distributed.

The second half of the century saw violent changes. In 745 B.C. Tiglath Pileser came to the throne of Assyria, and under him there was a great resurgence of Assyrian power. In the north the long reign of Jeroboam (he died in about 742) was followed by a rapid succession of kings, many of whom came to violent ends. In 722 Samaria, the capital, fell to the Assyrians. Israel had tumbled in twenty years from the high point of her prosperity and power to the status of a vassal, deprived not only of her independence but almost of her national identity.

In Judah things were somewhat better. Uzziah's immediate

I

successors wisely gave in to Assyrian pressure. But when Hezekiah, nearer the end of the century, reversed this policy and attempted to play an independent role, there was trouble for her too. But this takes us beyond our period.

Relations between Israel and Judah at this time appear to have been good, though they had not always been. Possibly Israel was still very much the senior partner. At any rate Israel was the wealthier, the stronger, the more sophisticated and culturally the more developed of the two.

The two peoples do seem to have felt that they were in some sense one. Hosea often talks of them as such, and seems to have regarded the union of the two as the ideal state of affairs. There was nothing to prevent Amos, a southerner, from appearing in the northern cities of Bethel and Samaria and prophesying there.

WHEN DID AMOS PROPHESY?

Amos took up his prophetic career very near the middle of the century. The title of the book (1:1) mentions no other northern king but Jeroboam (died 742 B.C.), and Amos is usually placed at or near the end of his reign. It is clear from the book's contents that Israel's great era of prosperity is still in full swing, and it seems to be implied that there is as yet no obvious threat to it. Amos, though confidently prophesying doom, seems reluctant to specify the means whereby the doom will be brought about. In this case Amos' prophetic ministry probably antedates the rise of Tiglath Pileser in 745.

The length of Amos' ministry

There is a general tendency to assume that Amos' prophetic career was short. Most scholars think of it as not more than a few months. The likelihood is that the clash with Amaziah (7:10–17) brought Amos' public activities in the north to an abrupt conclusion. The dating of the prophecies 'two years before the earthquake' (1:1) would appear to confine them within a single year, unless the date is intended as the date at which the ministry began. The observation that all the recorded words of Amos could have been delivered in a matter of hours does not, of course, prove anything. So could the recorded words of Jesus.

One thing at least is clear. Amos' prophetic activity concentrates closely on a single issue. There is a relative lack of development in his thinking and an unwillingness to take in side issues. This suggests a short period of activity.

Nevertheless there is *some* development. There is, perhaps, evidence of two phases in his thinking, a phase in which Amos made conditional threats, appealed for repentance, and interceded when that was not forthcoming, and a second phase in which he announced unconditional and total doom.

WHEN DID HOSEA PROPHESY?

It is manifest that in Hosea's time the prosperity is gone, the state is in the throes of dissolution. Though it is conceivable that his work began before Jeroboam's death (the title, 1:1, mentions Jeroboam, and only Jeroboam, among the northern kings), it is thus clear from the book's contents that the bulk of Hosea's ministry must have fallen within the disturbed years following Jeroboam's reign. The list of southern kings mentioned in 1:1, though perhaps not much reliance should be placed on it, prolongs his career into the reign of Hezekiah (715–687 B.C.). But the book reflects no knowledge of the fall of the Northern Kingdom in 722, and we are doubtless justified in locating Hosea's activities within the third quarter of the eighth century, i.e. between 750 and 725. The record of the prophet's relations with his wife and family suggest that his career occupied a number of years, but we cannot say how many.

3

WHEN DID MICAH PROPHESY?

Micah's career, which was carried on in the south, unlike that of Amos and Hosea, seems to have begun before the fall of Samaria in 722 B.C. and to have continued after it. The title, which is again not to be trusted very far, mentions the reigns of Jotham (742–735), Ahaz (735–715) and Hezekiah (715–687). Micah is therefore partly contemporary with the northern prophet Hosea, as he is also partly contemporary with Isaiah of Jerusalem in the south.

WHAT IS A PROPHET?

It is all too easy to cast the men of the Old Testament in roles we are familiar with, to see Amos, for example, as a kind of social reformer. Up to a point this may help us to understand them, but it is also dangerous, for we may end up *mis*understanding them instead.

Any healthy society needs its critics, and the prophets performed this function. In our own society the same function is fulfilled by the press, by the parliamentary opposition and by all sorts of consumer organizations and citizens' councils. But the prophet is far more than all or any of these. He is first and foremost a man of God. He is a religious visionary. His criticisms therefore were felt to have a force and authority with which we should not credit the criticisms of any modern functionary, and our society, therefore, offers no real parallel to his office.

It is also easy to see the prophet as an innovator, as an original thinker, impressing his own new moral insights on society and arriving at fresh ideas about religion. It would be a mistake to discount the originality of the prophets altogether, but assuredly this is not how they saw themselves. The prophet sees himself as the bearer of a tradition. He judges society by a set of standards received from the past. He is at once the most truly radical and the most truly conservative of men, for the

4

most disturbing radicalism is that which demands that we take seriously the ancient beliefs which we already profess to hold, and put into practice the principles to which ostensibly we already adhere. The man who does demand that society take its professed beliefs with absolute seriousness, whether these beliefs be enshrined in the Sinai covenant or the Sermon on the Mount, is apt to appear simplistic, and this is how the prophets often appear.

But though the prophet is a man of God, and delivers what he believes to be a divine message, this does not mean that we are obliged to accept him or his word entirely at his own valuation. It does not prevent us from recognizing the more mundane influences which have coloured his thinking. When we hear Amos conveying God's indignation against the un-righteousness of Samaria, we can hardly help seeing it also as the expression of a countryman's disgust at what he regards as the vices of the town. And our acceptance of the prophet as inspired of God must not induce us to cloak the fact that he is a man of his time and shares the presuppositions of his time; presuppositions that we cannot always share with him. All the prophets, for example, accept a moralizing view of history which most modern men cannot regard as satisfactory.

WHAT IS DIFFERENT ABOUT THE EIGHTH-CENTURY PROPHETS?

The eighth-century prophets are different from earlier prophets first, and most obviously, in that earlier prophets did not have their words written down at length. Why did this happen to those of the eighth century?

It seems that the eighth-century prophets, while adhering to the traditions received from the past, drew certain conclusions from those traditions which their contemporaries found surprising.

The ancient tradition was that Yahweh (on the name Yahweh see p.13) had not always been the God of Israel.

He had adopted her and made a carefully defined agreement with her on Sinai (a 'covenant'). This agreement was confirmed at Shechem after the entry into Canaan. In the agreement God appears as a rather stern and inflexible character who insists rigidly on the keeping of the agreed conditions. Josh. 24: 19 states unambiguously, 'He is a holy god, a jealous god, and he will not forgive your rebellion and your sins...he will make an end of you.'

The eighth-century prophets deduce from this that, since Israel has manifestly not fulfilled the conditions of the covenant, God will destroy her. Since he managed without her before the agreement was made, he could presumably do so again. There is therefore no reason why he should not destroy her totally.

The prophets' contemporaries found this surprising, first, because it was by no means as obvious to them as to the prophets that they were not fulfilling the terms of the covenant. They interpreted their religious obligations more liberally. But more important, the tradition of the conditional covenant had been overlaid in their minds by more comforting notions. They saw in the presence of the divinely appointed king, and in the presence of God himself with them in the sanctuary, the guarantees of divine favour. That God could punish them if they displeased him they did not doubt, but that he should totally and finally destroy them they found unthinkable. Moreover, they must have seen their prosperity during the first half of the eighth century as evidence that God was anything but displeased.

Now as far as the Northern Kingdom was concerned, the predictions of the prophets were fulfilled to the letter, and within the prophets' own lifetime or shortly afterwards. They were fulfilled while there were still plenty of people around who could remember what they said. Their words were therefore treated with respect and eventually written down, for the dire conclusion which they had drawn from the old traditions seemed to be abundantly confirmed by events.

THE MATERIALS OF THE PROPHETIC BOOKS

The most prominent type of literary material in prophetic books is the poetic oracle. Poetic oracles may stand alone or in short series. When standing alone they may have a brief narrative framework, describing the event that called them forth. When they appear in series we have to decide whether they were so arranged by the prophet himself or by his editors. How we decide this question will make a difference to the interpretation we place on them. Sometimes oracles in similar form are scattered throughout a prophetic book, and we deduce that they may once have been a series which is now broken up.

Occasionally an oracle may appear twice in different forms, perhaps as a poetic oracle and then as a prose summary. From this we may deduce that it has been handed down by at least two different groups of people, who may each have set their own stamp on it. The fact that the book of Amos, for example, provides no instances of this phenomenon argues for a short and uncomplicated phase of oral transmission. That is to say, there was only a short period before the material was written down, and during which it was passed on by word of mouth. The apparent duplication of 2: 6 and 8: 6 is not a real exception; see note on 8: 6.

Oracles themselves fall into different types. There are judgement oracles pronounced on individuals, and judgement oracles on communities. Both types abound in the books with which we are concerned. Salvation oracles, on the contrary, hardly occur at all in Amos, but are more abundant in Hosea and still more so in Micah.

Oracular material may sometimes be modelled on forms of speech which properly belong to other areas of life. A prophet may deliver his address in the style of a lament (a kind of premature obituary), for example, or in the manner of counsel for the prosecution making a formal accusation. Or he may deliberately adopt the style of a sanctuary prophet and pronounce a solemn execration, a cursing of the enemies of God.

7

We are often aware that a fresh oracle is beginning because of the introductory formula which stands at its head. Examples of such formulae are, 'Hear the word of the LORD', 'These are the words of the LORD', or 'Hear this word'. It is important for our interpretation to know where an oracle begins and ends.

Descriptions of visions comprise another common class of material, and the visions themselves can be classified into a number of varieties.

In addition, we have biographical and autobiographical material. This is of the greatest interest to us, but we have to realize at once that the early collectors of the traditions were certainly not interested in it for its own sake. It is included only where it is strictly relevant to the message. Perhaps the commonest autobiographical accounts in the prophets are accounts of the call. These are common because the call constitutes, at least for the prophet himself, his authority to speak. He tends to refer to his call, therefore, when his authority is challenged, though even then he may do so very cryptically.

THE STRUCTURE OF THE PROPHETIC BOOKS

Amos

What part did Amos play in the composition of the book which bears his name? A whole range of views is still possible. Some are prepared to argue that Amos composed it virtually as it stands. Other scholars, at the opposite extreme, reckon with a long period of oral transmission which would leave no possibility that Amos had a hand in the writing. Such scholars do, however, insist on the accuracy and dependability of oral tradition and assert that we nevertheless possess many of the actual words of Amos.

A number of attempts have been made to identify two 'books of Amos' which have been put together to make our present one: e.g. a 'book of visions' and a 'book of words'; or, a book containing both visions and historical sections, and a book of oracles only; or, a book of speeches delivered by the prophet before his expulsion by Amaziah, and a book of later speeches and visions. The scholars who advance these analyses sometimes ascribe to Amos an active part in the compilation, and see him as retiring, after his dismissal from Bethel, to a southern sanctuary to edit his prophecies and wait for their fulfilment. The failure of the exponents of the two-book theories to agree in their reconstructions of the two books does not inspire confidence in analysis of this sort.

The view taken in this commentary is that Amos is responsible not merely for the individual oracles but for the arrangement of many of them into series: i.e. he delivered some of them, orally, in series, but is unlikely to have written them down. We therefore have to reckon with a short period of oral transmission. The present ordering of the series and of the other materials in the book is due to those who handed the materials on. The bulk of the book is likely to have been collected in a single operation shortly after 722 B.C., when events seemed to have justified Amos' predictions. The hopeful prophecies at the end of the book, and a few other small passages, were added later. Some additions and minor changes were made by a Judaean editor, for at some stage the book was taken over by the southern community and adapted to their needs.

Several prophetic books seem to have grown by a process of accretion, passing through a period in which an original body of written material was supplemented from a still living body of oral tradition. Few traces of such a process can be discerned in the book of Amos. There is an almost total lack of duplicate or overlapping material, and a concentration of the subject-matter on a single theme. Books which have grown by accretion are unlikely to exhibit these features.

Hosea

The book of Hosea falls into two parts. Chapters 1–3 are concerned with the prophet's marriage and the message he derived from it. The variation between first person ('I') and third person ('he') styles shows that these chapters were not originally a single, continuous account. Chapters 4–14 are a mixed bag of oracles, mostly oracles of judgement. There is little discernible pattern in the collection, oracles being linked largely by catchwords, though sometimes by similarity of content. This suggests that Hosea himself was not responsible for bringing them together. Catchword links are characteristic of oral transmission.

The text of Hosea

Attention must be drawn at the outset to the fact that the text of Hosea has been very badly preserved. Many lines, or whole verses, of the Hebrew text as we now have it are very obscure, and sometimes they are complete nonsense. Often we can make a reasonable guess as to what was originally written, but sometimes we have to admit that the meaning is irrecoverable. The notes to the N.E.B. indicate a number of points at which obscurities exist, and the commentary indicates yet more, but neither notes nor commentary has space to catalogue all the difficulties. The poor state of the text also explains why there are so many places in Hosea where different translators produce wildly different translations.

The reader might easily gain the impression from this that the biblical text is largely incomprehensible even to the experts, and that biblical translation and interpretation are hazardous enterprises. This is not so. Most Old Testament books contain obscure passages, but in most cases they are relatively few. Hosea is altogether exceptional in the severity of its textual problems.

Micah

The book of Micah, in complete contrast from that of Amos, must have grown up over a long period. It contains collections of the words of the eighth-century prophet, but these have been substantially added to in later generations. The book cannot have achieved its present form until after the Babylonian exile, which started in 586 B.C.

The book falls readily into three parts. Chapters 1–3 are made up of oracles denouncing the sins of Judah and Samaria, and are mostly authentic oracles of Micah. Chapters 4–5 are composed almost entirely of oracles of salvation, and nearly all of these were produced after Micah's day. Chapters 6–7 are a mixture of oracles of different types and different dates; some of them, no doubt, by Micah himself. The dates of the individual oracles, and the criteria we use for assessing them, are discussed in the body of the commentary.

✻   ✻   ✻   ✻   ✻   ✻   ✻   ✻   ✻   ✻   ✻   ✻   ✻

AMOS

✻   ✻   ✻   ✻   ✻   ✻   ✻   ✻   ✻   ✻   ✻   ✻   ✻

1 THE WORDS OF AMOS, one of the sheep-farmers of
Tekoa, which he received in visions concerning Israel
during the reigns of Uzziah king of Judah and Jeroboam
son of Jehoash king of Israel, two years before the earthquake. He said,

2
The LORD roars from Zion
and thunders from Jerusalem;
the shepherds' pastures are scorched
and the top of Carmel[a] is dried up.

THE TITLE AND INTRODUCTION

✻ Verse 1 is the title to the book. Its rather clumsy construction suggests that it has been expanded, perhaps in several
stages.

We shall look more closely at the question of Amos' profession when we consider the account of his call in chapter 7,
but if he was a *sheep-farmer* he is likely to have been a semi-
nomad, i.e. a tent-dweller who moved on from time to time,
but on a fixed and somewhat restricted circuit. In this case he
would belong to *Tekoa* only in the sense that he was centred
on that region, much as Abraham is described in Genesis as
belonging to the city of Ur. According to 7: 14, Amos was
also 'a dresser of sycomore-figs'. Since these do not grow at
the altitude of Tekoa he cannot have spent all his time there.

Palestine has always had a sizeable semi-nomadic population. Such people may be culturally isolated from urban
civilization, but they are geographically very close to it and
well informed about it. Tekoa is on the edge of the desert, but

[a] top of Carmel: *or* choicest farmland.

12

Jerusalem is a mere twelve miles away to the north. The semi-nomads of ancient Israel (like those of modern Islam) were conservative in religion and puritan in morals. It is from such a background that Amos came to the sophisticated city of Samaria. Amos is a puritan, and unless we begin with a fundamental respect for puritanism we shall fail to do him justice.

Amos' words are *concerning Israel*. It is possible that 'Israel' here, and elsewhere in the book, means the whole country, north and south together (cp. 3: 1 and 6: 1), but for the most part Amos appears as a man with a limited mission. He is sent to one place, the Northern Kingdom. He has a short time to speak. And he only has one thing to say.

The earthquake is also mentioned in Zech. 14: 5, a passage written about four centuries later than Amos, and is there dated in the reign of Uzziah. Earthquakes are frequent in Palestine and this must have been a big one to be thus worthy of mention. It is possible that the earthquake, coming so soon after Amos had spoken, was taken as the first confirmation of the truth of his message and first stimulated people to recall his oracles.

Verse 2 is a snatch of poetry. It does not properly belong either to the title or to what follows. It has parallels in Joel 3: 16 and Jer. 25: 30 and is echoed in the Psalms and elsewhere. It is probably a fragment of a hymn used in the Jerusalem temple and placed here when the book of Amos was taken over for use in public worship or re-applied to the needs of Judah. There is no other suggestion in the book that Amos had any special attachment to Jerusalem or its temple.

The LORD: wherever the word 'LORD' appears in the N.E.B. Old Testament, printed in capitals, it represents the divine name, which was probably pronounced 'Yahweh'. From quite early times the Jews held the name in such reverence that when they read the scriptures they refrained from pronouncing it, substituting instead some other title, such as 'the Lord'. Most translators of the Old Testament, both ancient and modern, have followed Jewish tradition in this matter and have not tried to reproduce the name itself. *

13

The sins of Israel and her neighbours

At times of national conflict prophets and soothsayers were regularly called on to proclaim God's blessing on the cause. See, for example, the instance of Balaam in Num. 22–4, and the four hundred prophets appealed to by Ahab in 1 Kings 22. And even in times of peace there were national occasions on which it was felt appropriate to ask God not only to bless his people but to curse their enemies. Amos' solemn execration of the nations may have been uttered on such an occasion; perhaps at the Autumn Festival (cp. comments on 5: 16–27).

Amos is doing what was expected of prophets at such times. His execration is delivered in stereotyped phrases. He curses the traditional enemies (they were not all a real threat to Israel at the time when he spoke). He is following a well-known formula. But there is an unexpected twist at the end.

The judgement pronounced is in every case a judgement by fire (cp. 7: 4–6). The fire is a symbol of the divine wrath, especially as made manifest in war. The imagery throughout is war imagery, but the human agent is never hinted at. Whatever the human agent, the real enemy is God.

All Amos' execrations are pronounced for moral offences. Not all the offences are ones committed against Israel. Amos assumes that God is concerned with the doings of all nations, and that all are responsible to the same moral law.

3 These are the words of the LORD:

> For crime after crime of Damascus
>> I will grant them no reprieve,
> because they threshed Gilead under threshing-sledges
>> spiked with iron.

Therefore will I send fire upon the house of Hazael, 4
fire that shall eat up Ben-hadad's palaces;
　　I will crush the great men of Damascus　　5
and wipe out those who live in the Vale of Aven
　　and the sceptred ruler of Beth-eden;
the people of Aram shall be exiled to Kir.
　　It is the word of the LORD.

These are the words of the LORD:　　6

For crime after crime of Gaza
　　I will grant them no reprieve,
because they deported a whole band of exiles
　　and delivered them up to Edom.
Therefore will I send fire upon the walls of Gaza, 7
　　fire that shall consume its palaces.
I will wipe out those who live in Ashdod　　8
　　and the sceptred ruler of Ashkelon;
I will turn my hand against Ekron,
　　and the remnant of the Philistines shall perish.
　　It is the word of the Lord GOD.

These are the words of the LORD:　　9

For crime after crime of Tyre
　　I will grant them no reprieve,
　　because, forgetting the ties of kinship,
they delivered a whole band of exiles to Edom.
　　Therefore will I send fire upon the walls of Tyre, 10
　　fire that shall consume its palaces.

THE ORACLE AGAINST DAMASCUS (I: 3–5)

✴ Damascus was the capital, then as now, of Syria (called Aram in Hebrew and in the N.E.B.). Israel's territories across Jordan, of which *Gilead* was the richest, were always exposed to attack when Syria was strong. The events mentioned here probably took place when Hazael conquered the region, about fifty years before Amos' time (2 Kings 10: 32–3, 8: 11–12, 13: 3–7).

threshing-sledges of a number of different types were used, but the principle of all of them was the same. An animal would pull the sledge round and round over the grain, while men continually threw the sheaves afresh into its path. Arab peasants still use the method, though nowadays the sledge is often a sheet of corrugated iron.

4. *Hazael* was the founder of the reigning dynasty (2 Kings 8: 7–15) and *Ben-hadad* ('son-of-Hadad') was a common name among the Syrian kings, Hadad being the national deity.

5. *the Vale of Aven* is the region of what is now called Baalbek, between Lebanon and Anti-Lebanon. Several possible sites for *Beth-eden* have been suggested. The location of *Kir* is not known. According to 9:7 it is where the Syrians originally came from.

Amos may have lived to see this prophecy come true. Damascus fell to the Assyrians in 732 B.C. ✴

THE ORACLE AGAINST GAZA (I: 6–8)

✴ Gaza represents all Philistia, as Damascus represents Syria, but the other major Philistine cities, with the exception of Gath, do receive mention. The omission of Gath is odd. It did exist in Amos' time, for we have accounts of how the Assyrians destroyed it in 711 B.C. To some scholars the omission suggests that the oracle is a later invention, added after 711, but such a conclusion seems unnecessary. See also the note on 9: 7.

We do not know to what incident Amos is referring when he says *they deported a whole band of exiles*. It may simply be an allusion to regular slave-trading activities. ✳

THE ORACLE AGAINST TYRE (I : 9–10)

✳ It is possible that the phrase *ties of kinship*, literally 'covenant of brothers', refers to the old covenant between Hiram of Tyre and king Solomon (1 Kings 5). Or it might refer to the later covenant between Sidon and northern Israel which was cemented by the marriage of Ahab and Jezebel (1 Kings 16: 29–31). Otherwise it may not relate to Israel at all, but to some other nation with which Tyre was in league.

The authenticity of this oracle has been suspected on the grounds that it is so similar to the previous one. But if Amos is using a stereotyped pattern of denunciation, and has little of which to accuse Tyre except complicity in the slave trade, he might have uttered it in this form. The question must remain open. ✳

These are the words of the LORD:

> For crime after crime of Edom   11
>   I will grant them no reprieve,
> because, sword in hand, they hunted their kinsmen
>   down,
>   stifling their natural affections.
> Their anger raged unceasing,
> their fury stormed unchecked.
> Therefore will I send fire upon Teman,   12
> fire that shall consume the palaces of Bozrah.

These are the words of the LORD: 13

> For crime after crime of the Ammonites
>   I will grant them no reprieve,

because in their greed for land
they invaded the ploughlands of Gilead.

14 Therefore will I set fire to the walls of Rabbah,
fire that shall consume its palaces
amid war-cries on the day of battle,
with a whirlwind on the day of tempest;

15 then their king shall be carried into exile,
he and his officers with him.
It is the word of the LORD.

2 These are the words of the LORD:

For crime after crime of Moab
I will grant them no reprieve,
because they burnt the bones of the king of Edom
to ash.[a]

2 Therefore will I send fire upon Moab,
fire that shall consume the palaces in their towns;
Moab shall perish in uproar,
with war-cries and the sound of trumpets,

3 and I will cut off the ruler from among them
and kill all their officers with him.
It is the word of the LORD.

THE ORACLE AGAINST EDOM (1: 11–12)

✻ This oracle comes from a later hand than Amos'. It fits
perfectly into the situation after Judah's fall in 586 B.C. This
period, in which many Jews were taken into exile in Babylon,
we refer to as the exilic period. In the exilic period Edom took
advantage of Judah's weakness and the Jews felt deep bitter-
ness about this. Accusations against Edom of the sort made

[a] to ash: *or* for lime.

here are not found in pre-exilic texts, though they do occur in some post-exilic ones (e.g. Obadiah). The oracle therefore does not fit the eighth century at all. Up to the eighth century Edom had suffered more atrocities at Israel's hands than she inflicted, as far as our records go (see, e.g., 1 Kings 11: 14–16). *

THE ORACLE AGAINST AMMON (1: 13–15)

* The territory of Ammon was across Jordan. The *Rabbah* mentioned in verse 14 is present-day Amman. The attack on *Gilead* probably happened when Israel was under pressure from the Syrians towards the end of the previous century.

14. The *whirlwind on the day of tempest* may be a metaphor for the onslaught of the attacking armies, but more likely this is the tempest which accompanies the appearances of God. This onslaught is a divine rather than an entirely natural one.

15. *their king* (Hebrew *malkam*) is perhaps a play on words. 'Milkom' was the name of the Ammonite god. *

THE ORACLE AGAINST MOAB (2: 1–3)

* Moab lies to the east of the Dead Sea. The incident here complained of is not recorded elsewhere. There is no good reason to connect it with the attack on Moab which is recounted in 2 Kings 3, though this account, and the one given on the Moabite Stone, show that hostilities between the two countries were common. The Moabite Stone is a ninth-century inscription by Mesha, king of Moab. For further details see the volume in this series, *The Making of the Old Testament.*

To pursue the dead, even to the point of violating the corpse, is a mark of peculiar hatred and peculiarly offensive to the common conscience of mankind.

2. The word rendered *their towns* might equally readily be taken as a place name, Qeriyyoth, which is mentioned on the Moabite Stone. *

4 These are the words of the LORD:

> For crime after crime of Judah
> I will grant them no reprieve,
> because they have spurned the law of the LORD
> and have not observed his decrees,
> and have been led astray by the false gods
> that their fathers followed.
5 Therefore will I send fire upon Judah,
> fire that shall consume the palaces of Jerusalem.

THE ORACLE AGAINST JUDAH

* This oracle at its beginning and end conforms to the pattern of the others, though compared with the others its prediction of punishment is very bare and unspecific. But the middle of the oracle, specifying Judah's crimes, is not at all characteristic of Amos, either in what it says or the language in which it says it. Amos elsewhere does not show a great deal of interest in irregularities in worship (being *led astray by the false gods*) or in *the law of the LORD* and *his decrees*.

For this reason the whole oracle is suspected of being a later fabrication. But could Amos have left Judah out? We may take it that he probably did deliver an oracle on Judah, but not in these terms. The middle of Amos' original oracle has been replaced by someone who could not imagine a prophet condemning Judah except on the basis of the law, and could not believe that he would ignore Judah's chief weakness, for *false gods*. *

6 These are the words of the LORD:

> For crime after crime of Israel
> I will grant them no reprieve,
> because they sell the innocent for silver
> and the destitute for a pair of shoes.

They grind[a] the heads of the poor into the earth   7
  and thrust the humble out of their way.
Father and son resort to the same girl,
  to the profanation of my holy name.
  Men lie down beside every altar   8
    on garments seized in pledge,
  and in the house of their God[b] they drink liquor
    got by way of fines.

Yet it was I who destroyed the Amorites before them,[c] 9
  though they were tall as cedars,
  though they were sturdy as oaks,
  I who destroyed their fruit above
    and their roots below.
It was I who brought you up from the land of Egypt, 10
I who led you in the wilderness forty years,
  to take possession of the land of the Amorites;
  I raised up prophets from your sons,   11
    Nazirites from your young men.
  Was it not so indeed, you men of Israel?
    says the LORD.
  But you made the Nazirites drink wine,   12
and said to the prophets, 'You shall not prophesy.'
  Listen, I groan under the burden of you,   13
  as a wagon creaks under a full load.
  Flight shall not save the swift,   14
  the strong man shall not rally his strength.
  The warrior shall not save himself,
  the archer shall not stand his ground;   15
  the swift of foot shall not be saved,

[a] They grind: *prob. rdg., cp. Sept.; Heb. obscure.*   [b] *Or* gods.   [c] *Or, with some MSS.,* you.

21

nor the horseman escape;

16   on that day the bravest of warriors

shall be stripped of his arms and run away.

This is the very word of the LORD.

THE ORACLE AGAINST ISRAEL

✴ Having pronounced his execrations on the nations, Amos turns to Israel. From God's point of view she too is the enemy. It is possible that the prophets did sometimes end their execrations by cursing individuals in their own camp, but we can be sure that outright condemnation of the entire home nation was unprecedented. The condemnations of foreign peoples were meant to be the precursor to salvation oracles uttered on Israel. The new thing that Amos does is to include her in the judgement.

The oracle is in the same style as the rest, but is much expanded. Instead of picking out just one sin, as in the other cases, Amos gives us a catalogue. He also introduces a new element in the shape of a recitation of what Israel owes to God (verses 9–11). Her offences are not against the rules of common humanity, but against her covenant God and his requirements. The punishment, too, is described at greater length. It is not simply, 'And I will send fire...' Nevertheless, though expressed in different words, the theme is still that of judgement by warfare.

6. *For crime after crime of Israel:* instead of picking out an atrocity committed by nation against nation, Amos turns to the more domestic offences with which he is familiar, committed by Israelite against Israelite. *the innocent:* literally 'the righteous'. The N.E.B. rightly gives the word the technical force which it had in judicial contexts. It is the corruption of justice that Amos is concerned with here. *a pair of shoes:* a shoe was a token of property. To hand over a sandal was to make a token payment or deposit. When land was sold, since it could not literally be 'handed over', a sandal was handed over

in token (cp. Ruth 4: 7). Amos is making ironic reference to
such practices.

7. *and thrust the humble out of their way* may be an idiomatic
expression for 'deprive them of their legal rights'. *Father and
son resort to the same girl* sounds like an accusation of promis-
cuity. But the Hebrew contains no word for 'same'. It is
possible that the girl is a cult prostitute, but there is more to be
said for a recent suggestion that she is a household servant.
The men take advantage of her and treat her as a family concubine. 'Father and son sleep with the maid.' This fits in with
Amos' theme of oppression of the underprivileged.

8. *garments seized in pledge* are those held as surety for debt.
If a man has no surety other than his clothing he must be very
poor. The rule in Exod. 22: 26 is that such clothing must not
be held overnight.

Deeply rooted in Israelite tradition, and especially prophetic
tradition, is the idea of God as the protector of the poor, who
will avenge wrongs done to those whom no human court will
vindicate.

Amos is a man of fierce and narrow concentration. Even
his condemnations are mainly focused on one area of life,
on social justice. He shows little interest in purely religious
offences. Hosea, only a short while afterwards, found Israel
indulging in apostasy on a grand scale. Amos virtually ignores it.

We are perhaps too ready to assume that the Israel of Amos'
day was outstanding in corruption. But we are seeing it
through a puritan's eyes, and a puritan's view of any society
is never flattering. A civilized Israelite would have felt that
there was much to be proud of in Jeroboam's Israel. But to
Amos there is only one standard by which a society is judged,
not by its economic prosperity or the extent of its political
influence, but by the way it treats its poor.

9–12. There may have been special occasions on which the
Israelites, in their public worship, reminded themselves of
their covenant with God and perhaps undertook to renew that
covenant. A standing feature of such celebrations would be

the recital of God's mighty acts. These verses echo such recitals. Either Amos himself is using the familiar language of the cult or some later person who passed on his words has added this catalogue of mighty acts because he thought, rightly, that it was appropriate to Amos' theme.

9. The legend that the pre-Israelite inhabitants of Palestine were *tall as cedars*, or otherwise of gigantic size, is widespread in the Old Testament (e.g. Num. 13: 32–3).

11. The *Nazirites* were a curious, and ancient, institution. They were men especially devoted to the religious life. As an expression of this they refrained from cutting their hair and refused to *drink wine*. In later times the Nazirite vow was a temporary one (cp. Num. 6), but in the early period it seems to have been a lifelong profession, like Samson's.

12. *and said to the prophets, 'You shall not prophesy.'* Amos anticipates his own fate. He was not unique among prophets in being silenced.

Some commentators suggest that verse 10 ought to precede verse 9. This looks logical to us, but may not have appeared necessary to an ancient oriental.

Verse 13 is difficult, and other renderings have been proposed: 'I will cause the earth to totter under you', 'I will press you down in your place.' But some comparison to a loaded harvest cart is obviously intended. The agricultural image changes swiftly to an equally vivid picture of the panic-stricken flight of the defeated. ✳

Israel's sins and threatened punishment

PRIVILEGE AND RESPONSIBILITY

LISTEN, ISRAELITES, to these words that the LORD 3
addresses to you, to the whole nation which he brought
up from Egypt:

> For you alone have I cared   2
> among all the nations of the world;
> therefore will I punish you
> for all your iniquities.
>
> Do two men travel together   3
> unless they have agreed?
> Does a lion roar in the forest   4
> if he has no prey?
> Does a young lion growl in his den
> if he has caught nothing?
> Does a bird fall into a trap on the ground   5
> if the striker is not set for it?
> Does a trap spring from the ground
> and take nothing?
> If a trumpet sounds the alarm,   6
> are not the people scared?
> If disaster falls on a city,
> has not the LORD been at work?[a]
>
> For the Lord GOD does nothing   7
> without giving to his servants the prophets

[a] If disaster...work?: *or* If there is evil in a city, will not the LORD act?

knowledge of his plans.

8 The lion has roared; who is not terrified?
The Lord GOD has spoken; who will not prophesy?

✻ Verse 1 is a prose introduction which, unusually for Amos, addresses what follows *to the whole nation*, i.e. south as well as north.

Verse 2 is virtually a summary of Amos' entire message. He begins from the old traditions, which described how God chose Israel at the time of the exodus and made his covenant with her on Sinai. These old traditions make it clear that whoever accepts the covenant accepts exacting standards and puts himself under the service of a rigorous master. The statement of them in Josh. 24: 19–20 is unequivocal: 'He is a holy god, a jealous god, and he will not forgive your rebellion and your sins. If you forsake the LORD and worship foreign gods, he will turn and bring adversity upon you and, although he once brought you prosperity, he will make an end of you.' He who enters the covenant and then breaks it is thus worse off than if he had left it alone. In entering the sphere of grace he exposes himself in a peculiar way to divine judgement. This aspect of the covenant traditions had been conveniently forgotten by most of Amos' contemporaries. They were inclined to look on the covenant as the guarantee of God's protection.

2. *For you alone have I cared*: Amos concedes, for the sake of the argument, the particularistic viewpoint of his contemporaries. He puts the matter in different perspective later (9:7).

In verses 3–8 he throws at us a series of pictures. We must not try to see meaning in them individually. What matters is the total impact of the series. The meaning lies in what they have in common.

There are two possible lines of interpretation. First, the passage may be taken as a defence of Amos' right to prophesy. (On this theme see the comments on 7: 10–17.) On this interpretation the pictures are all instances of cause and effect. Moral: when God speaks, there is no gainsaying. The prophet cannot help himself; he has to say what he is told to say. *The Lord GOD has spoken; who will not prophesy?*

This interpretation makes good sense, but there is nothing in the present context to raise this issue, and if this is what the series originally meant the man who compiled the book manifestly did not appreciate the fact.

The second interpretation is that the pictures presented are all of phenomena from which obvious conclusions can be drawn. Two people meet in the desert; they must have arranged to do so. (A lone man in the waste avoids strangers, if he is wise. He does not greet them.) A lion roars. It must have caught something. A snare springs. Something must have set it off. A siren sounds. Something must be wrong. Faced with facts like these, any man can draw the right conclusions.

Well then, such being the nature of the covenant God, and such the moral corruption of this generation, the conclusion is equally inescapable. 'If there is evil in a city, will not the LORD act?' (N.E.B. note). When the Lord God speaks as clearly as this, any fool can prophesy. The merit of this interpretation is that it sees the images of verses 3–8 as filling out the meaning of verse 2, to which the passage is joined.

5. The bird-trap referred to is probably of a type known to us from Egyptian pictures. Two semi-circular frames, covered with netting, lie flat to the ground, side by side, until a bird touches the striker which is set between them. Then they spring up and meet, enclosing the bird.

Verse 7 does not fit into the argument. It is a prose gloss, or explanation, introduced by a scribe who placed a different interpretation on the passage, regarding it as a justification of the prophet's authority.

This passage tells us a good deal about the mentality of Amos. He assumes, first, that what looks like moral corruption *to him* is corruption by anybody's standards. He does not conceive of the possibility of disagreement about this. Second, he is prepared to argue from moral facts to political conclusions. 'You are wicked, therefore you will suffer disaster.' To

Amos this argument from morality seems so blindingly obvious and so totally convincing that he cannot regard those who reject it as anything but perverse. But Amos' contemporaries would have denied his premise. They did not think of themselves as wicked. Most modern men would deny the logic of the conclusion. It would be reassuring if history could be shown to exhibit a consistent moral purpose, but such a pattern is difficult to demonstrate convincingly. We can appreciate the prophets' moral and religious judgements, however, without applauding or defending their theory of history.

Even though the main point of the images is the inescapability of the conclusions which Amos is drawing, it is nevertheless characteristic of the prophet that all the pictures, except the first, are of lurking violence, hidden menace. ✷

THOROUGHGOING DESTRUCTION!

9   Stand upon the palaces in Ashdod
         and upon the palaces of Egypt,
         and proclaim aloud:
      'Assemble on the hills of Samaria,
         look at the tumult seething among her people
         and at the oppression in her midst;
10   what do they care for honesty
      who hoard in their palaces the gains of crime and
         violence?'
      This is the very word of the LORD.

11 Therefore these are the words of the Lord GOD:

      An enemy shall surround[a] the land;
      your stronghold shall be thrown down
         and your palaces sacked.

[a] shall surround: *prob. rdg.*; *Heb.* and round.

28

These are the words of the LORD: 12

> As a shepherd rescues out of the jaws of a lion
>   two shin bones or the tip of an ear,
> so shall the Israelites who live in Samaria be rescued
> like a corner of a couch or a chip from the leg of a bed.[a]
> Listen and testify against the family of Jacob.   13
> This is the very word of the Lord GOD, the God of
>   Hosts.

> On the day when I deal with Israel   14
>   for all their crimes,
>   I will most surely deal with the altars of Bethel:
> the horns of the altar shall be hacked off
>   and shall fall to the ground.
> I will break down both winter-house and summer- 15
>   house;
>   houses of ivory shall perish,
> and great houses be demolished.
>   This is the very word of the LORD.

* The multiplicity of introductory formulae (see p. 8) shows
that here we have a collection of three or four fragmentary
sayings: *This is the very word of the LORD* (three times); *Therefore these are the words...*; *These are the words of the LORD*.
   9. Instead of *Ashdod* we should probably read 'Assyria', as
the Septuagint does. The two words are similar in Hebrew
and easily confused. We then have an invitation to the two
great powers of the contemporary world to witness how
ripe is Samaria for destruction.
   Verses 9-10 are cast in the form of a public summons. Israel
is on trial, and her neighbours are being called to give evidence,
if they have evidence to offer, and to confirm the court's

[a] or a chip...bed: *prob. rdg.; Heb. obscure.*

judgement on the offender. The conclusion of this summons is in verse 13, and into the middle of it have been inserted an unrelated oracle announcing judgement by war (verse 11) and an equally unrelated saying in proverbial style (verse 12).

The precise translation of verse 12 is problematical, but the point which it makes is clear enough. It has sometimes been cited as evidence that Amos accepted the notion of the 'saving remnant'; the idea that something, however small, will survive the divine judgement and serve as the core of a restored community. In reality the point is exactly the opposite. Nothing will be saved that is worth saving.

The legal background to the saying is found in Exod. 22:13. A shepherd was accountable to the sheep-owner for any animal lost, unless he could prove that it was lost owing to circumstances beyond his control. Loss due to beasts of prey counted in this way as 'unavoidable'. So in such cases it was important for the shepherd to rescue enough of the carcass to prove the cause of death. This is the picture in Amos' mind. There will be enough left to serve as evidence of the catastrophe, and no more. The broken bedstead and the debris of its ivory inlay is just enough to bear witness, 'Here was a city.' So will the few pathetic refugees bear witness, 'We were once a nation.'

12. The *lion* is for Amos a potent symbol. Powerful, silently menacing, suddenly and violently destroying, striking terror with the sound of its voice, it is for him a parable of his severe God.

14. *Bethel* was the principal sanctuary of the Northern Kingdom. Samaria, though the political capital, was not much more than a century old, having been built by Omri, Ahab's father, on virgin ground. It is just possible that *Bethel* in this verse could refer not to the town, but to the god of the same name. *the horns of the altar* were projections at its four corners. The altar's sanctity seems to have resided peculiarly in them. By grasping them the offender could gain sanctuary, as Joab tried to do (1 Kings 1:50, 2:8). Perhaps this is what Amos is

thinking of. There will no longer be even this last resort for the fugitive Israel.

15. The *houses of ivory* were the luxurious houses decorated with ivory carvings, which were fashionable at this period. Archaeologists have found quantities of fragments of beautiful ivory inlays in eighth-century levels at Samaria. These fragments must be what was left when the city was sacked by the Assyrians in 722 B.C. Cp. the 'ivory beds' mentioned in 6: 4.

It is *houses* that Amos picks out for condemnation, houses of all sorts: *winter-house, summer-house, houses of ivory, great houses.* We have described Amos as a semi-nomad, and he displays the contempt that such men feel for settled life. To hear a modern gypsy spit out the word 'house' is to open a window into the nomad's soul.

When a man is called by God he is not cut loose from his cultural prejudices. When Amos rages as the man of God should against wickedness, his rage is mixed with a countryman's disgust at urban civilization, the scorn of the cultural reactionary for contemporary fashion and the puritan's uncomprehending indignation at what he sees as the vices of city life. ✳

THE UPPER-CLASS COWS OF SAMARIA

Listen to this,   **4**
you cows of Bashan who live on the hill of Samaria,
you who oppress the poor and crush the destitute,
who say to your lords, 'Bring us drink':
the Lord GOD has sworn by his holiness   2
that your time is coming
    when men shall carry you away on their shields[a]
    and your children in fish-baskets.
    You shall each be carried straight out   3
        through the breaches in the walls

[a] *Or* baskets.

and pitched on a dunghill.[a]

This is the very word of the LORD.

✳ There is something about fashionable upper-class women that brings out the venom in a puritan. They epitomize for him the most offensive vices of society. Isaiah reacts to them much as Amos does (Isa. 3: 16–4: 1).

1. *Bashan* was a very fertile area of the Transjordan, famous, amongst other things, for its fine cattle.

There are several translation problems in this short passage. The principal one is in the second half of verse 2. The words translated *shields* and *fish-baskets* are usually rendered 'hooks' and 'fish-hooks' respectively. Good arguments can be found for either rendering. The practice of putting hooks in the mouths of prisoners, barbarous as it sounds, does seem to be attested in 2 Chron. 33: 11 (cp. Isa. 37: 29 and Ezek. 29: 4, which may, however, both be metaphorical) and this is confirmed by Assyrian reliefs. The picture in the prophet's mind may therefore be of the captive women, cruelly hooked in line, being led out through the gaps in the partially demolished walls after the sack of the city. Alternatively, if the N.E.B.'s translation is correct, the picture is of the dead bodies of these women being carried out on large shields and in baskets to be unceremoniously dumped.

3. *the Harmon* (N.E.B. note): if the reading of the Hebrew manuscripts is correct, this is an unknown place-name. ✳

AMOS' BLACK MASS

In 4: 4-12 Amos satirizes a festival at Bethel. He takes three primary features of the ritual: the call to worship, the recital of God's mighty acts (see comment on 2: 9-10), and the theophany, the appearance of God in the sanctuary. He presents an offensive parody of the first (verses 4-5), turns the second upside down by reciting God's acts, not of salvation,

[a] a dunghill: *prob. rdg.; Heb.* the Harmon.

but of judgement (verses 6–11) and announces the third in all earnestness (verse 12). The appearance of God is no parody. This is real. Verse 13 probably did not belong to the original scheme.

> Come to Bethel – and rebel!   4
> Come to Gilgal – and rebel the more!
> Bring your sacrifices for the morning,
> your tithes within three days.
> Burn your thank-offering without leaven: 5
> announce, proclaim your freewill offerings;
> for you love to do what is proper, you men of Israel!
>   This is the very word of the Lord GOD.

* Amos, usually preoccupied with social justice, turns momentarily to religion. He makes no charges that Israel worships Baal or other deities. He says nothing of cultic prostitution or other such irregularities. His condemnation is in a sense more radical than that.

Amos represents those conservative sections of Israel who had always looked askance at the permanent shrines and re-garded the entire cult that was carried on there as an innovation. A tabernacle (a kind of sacred tent) had been good enough for their fathers in the wilderness; it should be good enough still. The adoption of habits of worship like those of the settled peoples was in their eyes the beginning of Israelite decadence.

With prophetic irony, therefore, Amos condemns the whole cult, from start to finish, as an act of rebellion, not be-cause it is directed towards other gods, but because, as we shall see later (5: 25), he believes it to be a kind of worship which God has never asked for.

4. There were a number of places bearing the name *Gilgal* (it means 'stone circle'). The one meant here is very likely the one near Jericho, an ancient and important shrine (see also

33

notes on Hos. 9: 15, 17). The translation *bring your sacrifices for the morning, your tithes within three days* is based on the assumption that it was established practice to bring an offering on the first day of the feast and to present tithes on the third. There is no evidence, however, that such was ever the custom. On this interpretation the prophet is satirizing the Israelites' punctiliousness. They *love to do what is proper* (verse 5). This reminds us of Jesus' condemnation of the Pharisees, who tithe 'mint and dill and cummin', exhibiting their religiosity by scrupulously and perhaps ostentatiously keeping the rules.

The Hebrew could also be translated as, 'Bring your sacrifices every morning, your tithes every three days.' This makes the saying an example of prophetic hyperbole. Private daily sacrifice would in reality have been a crippling extravagance. *Annual* sacrifice was the custom. And tithes were brought not every three days but every three years. If this rendering is correct, the issue is not one of punctiliousness but of excess. This time it is like those Pharisees who fasted twice in the week, whereas once was sufficient to satisfy the law.

5. *Burn your thank-offering without leaven*: the obvious translation of the Hebrew is 'with leaven', though the N.E.B.'s rendering of the preposition can be defended. 'With leaven' would be against the priestly rules as they are set out in Lev. 2: 11, but we cannot be certain that these rules were in force in northern Israel in Amos' day. ✳

6   It was I who kept teeth idle[a]
        in all your cities,
            who brought famine on all your settlements;
            yet you did not come back to me.
        This is the very word of the LORD.

7   It was I who withheld the showers from you
        while there were still three months to harvest.

[a] *Lit.* clean.

34

I would send rain on one city
and no rain on another;
rain would fall on one field,
and another would be parched for lack of it.
From this city and that, men would stagger to another 8
for water to drink, but would not find enough;
 yet you did not come back to me.
 This is the very word of the LORD.

I blasted you with black blight and red;   9
 I laid waste[a] your gardens and vineyards;
the locust devoured your fig-trees and your olives;
 yet you did not come back to me.
 This is the very word of the LORD.

I sent plague upon you like the plagues of Egypt; 10
 I killed with the sword
  your young men and your troops of horses.
 I made your camps stink in your nostrils;
 yet you did not come back to me.
 This is the very word of the LORD.

 I brought destruction amongst you   11
as God destroyed Sodom and Gomorrah;
you were like a brand snatched from the fire;
 yet you did not come back to me.
 This is the very word of the LORD.

Therefore, Israel, this is what I will do to you; 12
and, because this is what I will do to you,
 Israel, prepare to meet your God.

   [a] I laid waste: *prob. rdg.; Heb.* to increase.

35

✻ Verses 6–12 exhibit a fairly regular poetic structure, though it has perhaps been obscured by the activities of later editors. The poem is five times punctuated by the refrain: *Yet you did not come back to me. This is the very word of the LORD.* In verses 6–11 the experience of Israel is described as a series of punishments. It can hardly be accident that there are exactly seven of them. The ancients regarded seven as a round number.

Amos is setting out plainly his doctrine of discipline. The object of punishment is in the first place remedial. It is meant to turn men back to God, to compel good behaviour. But if men refuse to repent, God has no other expedient to resort to but total destruction. If discipline fails, everything fails. What his contemporaries found new and startling about Amos was his willingness to contemplate the possibility that God means what he says, and that total destruction might actually take place. It is perhaps true to say that for Amos all wrongdoing is, in the last resort, inexplicable. To his mind, both the conditions laid down in the covenant (see p. 6) and the lessons of history are so very, very clear that it is incredible that anyone should ignore them.

But to his contemporaries it was not so clear. They doubtless resented his repeated judgement. *Yet you did not come back to me.* As they saw it, they did not need to 'come back' to God, since they had never forsaken him. And as evidence of their devotion, they would no doubt have cited the same religious enthusiasm about which Amos is so scathing in verses 4–5.

7. *It was I who withheld the showers from you while there were still three months to harvest:* in Palestine there is normally no rain after the beginning of May. It is important, however, that the dry season should not begin too early. If the showers do not continue throughout March and April the grain does not fill out properly and ripens prematurely, and in ancient times it also meant that there was insufficient water to replenish the cisterns on which the population depended for its domestic

water through the summer. The description of the drought in verses 7–8 is somewhat laboured and not in Amos' usual terse style. This is one point at which we may detect the influence of a later hand.

When Amos compiles his catalogue of disasters he is not thinking of recent events, or even of particular calamities at all. This is clear from the tenses of the Hebrew verbs. Famine, drought, blighting of crops, locust plagues, epidemics, defeats and destructions were all catastrophes from which Israel had suffered repeatedly throughout her settled life.

In verse 12 we move on a step to the theophany, the appearance of God, or at least the warning of it. *Prepare to meet your God.* Amos confidently expects some dramatic act of judgement. This act will not be like the former ones, but will be final, and administered by God in person. ✻

A DOXOLOGY

It is he who forges the thunder[a] and creates the wind, 13
    who showers abundant rain on the earth,[b]
    who darkens the dawn with thick clouds
    and marches over the heights of the earth –
    his name is the LORD the God of Hosts.

✻ This verse is the first of three short hymn-like passages which appear in the book (the others are 5: 8 and 9: 5–6, but see also 8: 8). In the Hebrew they are not complete sentences. They are, rather, exclamations, outbursts, ascriptions of praise. Some see them as quotations from or fragments of a single hymn. Others regard them as separate compositions. We do not know for certain whether Amos composed them, in liturgical style; whether he quoted them

[a] thunder: *so Sept.; Heb.* mountains.
[b] who showers...earth: *prob. rdg.; Heb.* who tells his thoughts to mankind.

from an existing hymn; or whether they were added to the book after his day, by someone who edited the work for use in public worship.

It must be appreciated that if we do conclude that this verse, or any other in the book, was not spoken by the prophet himself, we are not necessarily reducing its value and certainly not dismissing it as insignificant.

The God of Hosts: the 'hosts' are the hosts of heaven, i.e. the angelic forces and/or the stars, etc. Cp. Josh. 5: 13–15, Judg. 5: 20, Ps. 148: 2–3. ✻

ISRAEL'S FUNERAL

5 Listen to these words; I raise a dirge over you, O Israel:

2   She has fallen to rise no more,
           the virgin Israel,
       prostrate on her own soil, with no one to lift her up.

3 These are the words of the Lord GOD:

       The city that marched out to war a thousand strong
           shall have but a hundred left,
       that which marched out a hundred strong
       shall have but ten men of Israel left.

✻ The two introductory formulae in 5: 1 and 5: 3a show that we have here two separate little poems. The first (verse 2) is a lament, a funeral dirge over the deceased Israel. There was a well-recognized metrical form in which such laments were written, and this little fragment is in exactly the correct style.

The first line of the second poem is in the same rhythm and this is perhaps why the compiler remembered it just at this point. It is not a lament but a prediction of defeat in war. In warfare it was common for prophets to sing taunt-songs, directed at the enemy and predicting his defeat (Isaiah does this in 2 Kings 19: 21–8), and the proper metre for these was the same as for the lament. Amos, however, is predicting defeat not for the enemy, but for his own side.

2. *the virgin Israel* is a not uncommon and somewhat stereo-typed title for the nation, perhaps used here in order to heighten the tragic feeling. The death of a virgin, or of a man who had no children, was regarded as peculiarly sad (cp. Judg. 11: 38, 2 Sam. 18: 18). ✲

COME AND WORSHIP

These are the words of the LORD to the people of Israel: 4

Resort to me, if you would live, not to Bethel; 5
go not to Gilgal, nor pass on to Beersheba;
    for Gilgal shall be swept away
    and Bethel brought to nothing.[a]
If you would live, resort to the LORD, 6
or he will break out against Joseph like fire,
fire which will devour Israel[b] with no one to quench
     it;
he who made the Pleiades and Orion, 8[c]
who turned darkness into morning
and darkened day into night,
    who summoned the waters of the sea
    and poured them over the earth,
who makes Taurus rise after Capella 9
and Taurus set hard on the rising of the Vintager[d] –
    he who does this, his name is the LORD.[e]

[a] nothing: *prob. rdg., cp. Sept.; Heb.* trouble (*the Heb. word* aven, *cp.* Beth-aven *in Hos. 4: 15; 5: 8; 10: 5*).
[b] *So one MS.; others* Bethel.
[c] *Verse 7 transposed to follow verse 9.*
[d] who makes...Vintager: *prob. rdg.; Heb.* who smiles destruction on the strong, and destruction comes on the fortified city.
[e] his...LORD: *transposed from end of verse 8.*

* 5. *Resort to me, if you would live* may be a priestly formula, calling men to worship at the shrine. By frequenting the sanctuaries an Israelite would have thought that he *was* 're-sorting to the Lord'. Amos' appeal to resort to the Lord and not to the sanctuaries must have sounded startling, rather like saying, 'Don't go to Church. Worship God instead' (cp. 4: 4). *Beersheba* was an old sanctuary in the far south of Judah. It had associations with the patriarchs. Its mention here shows that the pilgrim from northern Israel did not limit himself to the shrines in his own territory. It also shows that it is not only northern shrines of which Amos is critical. Whether in the north or the south what goes on in the sanctuaries is irrelevant to the service of God.

6. *Joseph* was in theory a single tribe, but from very early times it was split into two halves, Ephraim and Manasseh, each of which was important enough in its own right to acquire tribal status. Between them the two made up the bulk of northern Israel and controlled its richest areas. By the time of Amos tribal government had long been a thing of the past, but the term *Joseph* still comes naturally as a designation of the Northern Kingdom. Cp. the note on Hos. 4: 17–18.

Verses 8–9 are the second of the hymn fragments or doxologies (see note on 4: 13). This one interrupts the connection between verse 7 and verse 10, a connection which the N.E.B. has restored. This awkward insertion favours the theory that the hymn fragments were not composed or inserted by the prophet, but put in, almost at random, by an editor.

Verse 9 used to be a great puzzle, until it was recognized that the odd Hebrew words in it were the partly corrupted names of starry constellations. *

JUSTICE ON THE UNJUST

You that turn justice upside down[a]   7
and bring righteousness to the ground,
you that hate a man who brings the wrongdoer to court 10
and loathe him who speaks the whole truth:
for all this, because you levy taxes on the poor   11
and extort a tribute of grain from them,
though you have built houses of hewn stone,
    you shall not live in them,
though you have planted pleasant vineyards,
    you shall not drink wine from them.
For I know how many your crimes are   12
    and how countless your sins,
you who persecute the guiltless, hold men to ransom
and thrust the destitute out of court.
At that time, therefore, a prudent man will stay quiet, 13
for it will be an evil time.

Seek good and not evil,   14
    that you may live,
that the LORD the God of Hosts may be firmly on
    your side,
    as you say he is.
Hate evil and love good;   15
    enthrone justice in the courts;
it may be that the LORD the God of Hosts
will be gracious to the survivors of Joseph.

---

* It is difficult to decide how this passage should be broken
down into paragraphs or separate oracles. The normal pattern

[a] upside down: *prob. rdg.; Heb.* poison.

41

for prophetic judgement sayings is: accusation first, then sentence. If we look for this pattern verses 7–11 seem to be a natural unit. The accusation runs from verse 7 down to the words *and extort a tribute of grain from them*. The sentence is the rest of verse 11. This leaves verse 12 as another accusation, but without any corresponding sentence. Was it once joined to verses 16–17, which look like a sentence without any accompanying accusation?

The accusations throughout this passage are concerned with the maladministration of justice in the local courts.

7. It would probably be better to translate this verse as, 'Woe to those who turn justice to poison.' 'Poison' is suggested by the N.E.B. note. The Hebrew is actually 'wormwood', a nasty, bitter-tasting herb. Justice is such a mockery that the word leaves a nasty taste in the mouth. On 'Woe!' see the comment on 5: 18.

Righteousness has a wider meaning in Hebrew than in English. For us it means something like 'rectitude', a rather stuffy-sounding virtue. For the Israelite it included all that is implied in 'rectitude' and 'justice', but far more besides. It involved benevolence and kindness. The righteous man was one who protected the weak and vindicated the innocent. The word therefore had an altogether warmer feeling than it has in English.

10. *who brings the wrongdoer to court* is literally '...to the gate', the gate tower of the town being the place where the court normally sat. The court was composed of the elders of the town or village. Cp. Ruth 4: 1–2.

11. *you levy taxes on the poor* is sometimes rendered, 'you trample on...' or 'you prey upon...'. An otherwise unknown word lies at the bottom of this translation problem.

To build houses and *not live in them*, or to plant vineyards and *not drink wine from them* was felt to be a peculiarly bitter misfortune. To have laboured and not yet to have reaped the fruits of labour was regarded as sufficient reason for avoiding military call-up (Deut. 20: 5–6). The same fruitless labour is

42

listed in Deut. 28: 30 among the punishments for breaking the covenant with God.

Houses of hewn stone: most houses in Palestine were built of mud brick, except for the foundations, for which rough stone was used. The larger buildings of eighth-century Samaria, however, as archaeologists have discovered, were of excellently and accurately dressed stone, a very expensive building material at the time.

12. To *hold men to ransom* means, in this context, to accept bribes in order to procure a miscarriage of justice.

13. This verse is a manifestly later insertion. It is totally at variance with Amos' own attitudes. The one thing a prophet could not do was to *stay quiet* in *an evil time.* Some scribe, prompted perhaps by verse 10, wrote this prudential observation in the margin and it was later copied into the text.

14. *Seek good and not evil, that you may live,* closely echoes verses 5 and 6. The word rendered *seek* is there translated 'resort to'. Amos' contemporaries had so emasculated the original idea of the covenant with God that they believed it guaranteed them divine favour, that the Lord was *firmly on* their *side* regardless of how they behaved.

15. See the comment on 3: 12. The phrase *survivors of Joseph* implies no thought of a 'saving remnant'. It expresses the prophet's view of the pathetic state into which the nation has fallen. He is calling her 'poor old Israel'. His hearers would find this insulting. To their short-sighted view the country was still at the height of its power.

We are now moving into the second phase of God's dealings with Israel. Phase 1 was the phase of discipline. Repentance would still set matters right. But now there is no certainty that this offer is still open. Amos cannot promise that at this late hour repentance will have any effect. He can only say, *It may be.* ✳

THE LORD'S DAY

16 Therefore these are the words of the LORD the God
of Hosts:[a]

There shall be wailing in every street,
and in all open places cries of woe.
The farmer shall be called to mourning,
and those skilled in the dirge to[b] wailing;
17 there shall be lamentation in every vineyard;
for I will pass through the midst of you,
says the LORD.

18 Fools who long for the day of the LORD,
what will the day of the LORD mean to you?
It will be darkness, not light.
19 It will be as when a man runs from a lion,
and a bear meets him,
or turns into a house and leans his hand on the wall,
and a snake bites him.
20 The day of the LORD is indeed darkness, not light,
a day of gloom with no dawn.

21 I hate, I spurn your pilgrim-feasts;
I will not delight in your sacred ceremonies.
22 When you present your sacrifices and offerings
I will not accept them,
nor look on the buffaloes of your shared-offerings.
23 Spare me the sound of your songs:
I cannot endure the music of your lutes.
24 Let justice roll on like a river
and righteousness like an ever-flowing stream.

[a] So Sept.; Heb. adds the Lord.
[b] Prob. rdg.; Heb. places to before those skilled.

Did you bring me sacrifices and gifts,   25
  you people of Israel, those forty years in the wilderness?
    No! but now you shall take up   26
    the shrine of your idol king
    and the pedestals of your images,*a*
  which you have made for yourselves,
and I will drive you into exile beyond Damascus.   27

So says the LORD; the God of Hosts is his name.

* This passage is a unit, and it is concerned with worship
from start to finish: or more precisely, it is concerned with
the Autumn Festival. The Autumn Festival was a harvest
festival, celebrating the last of the three harvests in Palestine,
that of grapes, olives and other fruits. In the Southern Kingdom it was associated with the autumn equinox, and was a
festival of light. The dawn of the equinoctial day was a high
point in the celebrations, when the sun shone through the
eastern gate of the sanctuary into the innermost shrine. It
would not be surprising if the Autumn Festival at Bethel
were centred on the same themes.

Amos, in characteristic fashion, contradicts every expectation. Instead of festal excitement he predicts mourning (verses
16–17), and on the day of light there *will be darkness, not light*.
The Lord will not rise in splendour and cause his face to shine
into the sanctuary, for there will be *no dawn*.

The best commentary on verses 16–17 is the book of Joel.
Joel was written for an Autumn Festival when there was
nothing to celebrate, a harvest thanksgiving for a harvest
which failed. It shows how the celebrations were replaced
by official days of penitence and mourning. This is what
Amos in these verses is envisaging. The mourning he speaks
of is concerned with the failure of harvest, and especially

[a] *Prob. rdg.; Heb. adds* the star of your gods.

45

of the vintage, for it is specifically the *farmer* who is *called to mourning*, and the lamentation is to be made *in every vineyard*.

18. In the Hebrew this verse and 6: 1 (and possibly 5: 7) begin with the word 'Woe!'. These 'woe sayings' form a series, though the N.E.B. translation masks this fact. 'Woe!' was normally a way of beginning a funeral dirge. Only prophets pronounce woe over the living.

The phrase *day of the LORD* conjures up to our minds pictures of the end of the world and the last judgement. Such ideas were not thought of until long after Amos' time. It is not so much *the day of the LORD* as 'the Lord's Day', a religious occasion. Amos is saying that the festal day to which Israel looks forward will be a day of tragedy and not of joy. It is a day when they will be under judgement, but not in any sense that implies an end of the world.

19. This verse is typical of Amos, both in its insertion of a bit of country wisdom into a rhetorical passage, and in the nightmare quality of its imagery. The actions should probably be regarded as consecutive, though the N.E.B., by choosing to translate *or* rather than 'and' (in the phrase, *or turns into a house*), implies otherwise. It is like a man describing a bad dream. Running from a lion he meets a bear. In even greater panic he reaches the shelter of his house. A snake strikes at him from a crevice in the wall. Amos' pictures of judgement often have about them this element of the uncanny. Man by his injustice disrupts the divine order and releases malign forces which pursue him.

21. *I hate, I spurn your pilgrim-feasts* is thus not a change of subject. The prophet is simply widening his condemnations to take in the whole of Israel's way of worship.

22. *buffaloes* are unlikely to have been prominent in Palestine. The word more probably refers to the humped cattle typical of eastern countries.

24. Most of the streams in Palestine are 'wadis', i.e. they remain dry throughout the summer. *an ever-flowing stream* is

a rare and comforting thing, staining the brown summer landscape a miraculous green.

25. *Did you bring me sacrifices and gifts...those forty years in the wilderness?* An astonishing question, and framed so as to demand an astonishing answer, 'No!'. According to the traditions which we find in the Pentateuch the answer should be an emphatic 'Yes!'. The Pentateuch asserts that the sacrificial system was actually instituted in the wilderness, through the agency of Moses and Aaron. But Amos subscribes to a different tradition, that of the old, conservative, pastoral Israel. And Amos' tradition is historically the more accurate one, for the sacrificial system as Amos knew it, and as we know it from the Pentateuch, was in essence Canaanite, and was not adopted until after the settlement. Jeremiah knows this too (7: 21-2). The patriarchs did offer sacrifice from time to time, and the Israelites in the wilderness did celebrate the Passover. Amos would doubtless have admitted these reservations if they had been put to him. What he is disputing is the divine origin of the institution as it existed in his day.

The translation of verse 26 is problematical. If it is a reference to idolatry it is very rare in Amos. But it may not be one. It seems quite possible that in Amos' day, images of the Lord himself were used, and were not thought of as unorthodox. Amos is simply picturing the deportation of the people and its sacred objects without making any criticism of their legitimacy.

27. *I will drive you into exile beyond Damascus:* a curiously vague indication of the place of exile. Amos must have known that the only likely agents of the disaster he was foretelling were the Assyrians. Why does he not name them? There are two possible reasons. (1) He is not concerned with the mechanics of the disaster, only in proclaiming the certainty that it will take place. (2) This is an example of the oblique oracular style. Amos does have Assyria specifically in mind, and his hearers know this very well. ✶

THE SCENE IN SAMARIA

6   Shame on you who live at ease in Zion,
    and you, untroubled on the hill of Samaria,
      men of mark in the first of nations,
    you to whom the people of Israel resort!

2   Go, look at Calneh,
    travel on to Hamath the great,
      then go down to Gath of the Philistines –
    are you better than these kingdoms?
    Or is your[a] territory greater than theirs[b]?

3   You who thrust the evil day aside
    and make haste to establish violence.[c]

4   You who loll on beds inlaid with ivory
      and sprawl over your couches,
    feasting on lambs from the flock
      and fatted calves,

5   you who pluck the strings of the lute
  and invent musical instruments like David,

6   you who drink wine by the bowlful
      and lard yourselves with the richest of oils,
    but are not grieved at the ruin of Joseph –

7   now, therefore,
    you shall head the column of exiles;
      that will be the end of sprawling and revelry.

＊ In 4: 1–3 Amos said what he thought about the upper-class women. Now he condemns the entire ruling class; those who, in their own estimation, are the *men of mark in the first*

[a] *Prob. rdg.; Heb.* their.   [b] *Prob. rdg.; Heb.* yours.
[c] You...violence: *or* You who invoke the day of wrongdoing and bring near the sabbath of violence.

of nations. He gives us a picture of a decadent aristocracy, who are totally out of touch with the living conditions of those they govern, and *are not grieved at the ruin of Joseph.* They are also complacently unaware of the threat to their own existence. Amos' description of their behaviour and attitudes agrees closely with the picture of the northern aristocracy which Isaiah of Jerusalem presents, writing about twenty years later (Isa. 9: 9-10, 28: 1-13).

1. *Shame on you,* or 'Woe to you!'. See comment on 5:18. Amos has the northerners principally in mind, but his opening words address his condemnation not only to those *on the hill of Samaria* but also to those *who live at ease in Zion.* Amos' hatred is not for a nation, but for a class.

Verse 2 is difficult. The N.E.B.'s rendering involves some manipulation of the text but is probably justifiable. Why are these particular cities, *Calneh, Hamath* and *Gath,* picked out for comparison? They were not, as a group, especially close to Israel, especially large, or especially prosperous, as far as we know. The likeliest explanation is that they were ones which had fallen to the Assyrians already. The speaker is saying: 'These cities were as thriving and confident as you. Look at them now.' But if this interpretation is correct the verse must have been inserted after Amos' time, for in his day they were still independent. They fell to Assyria during the decades following.

4. On *beds inlaid with ivory* see the comments on 3: 15. The beds were not for sleeping in but for reclining at table. The older custom in Israel was to sit. Our present text is the earliest mention of the practice of reclining to eat; a practice which became general in later times. It was doubtless a foreign fashion and Amos is predictably contemptuous of it.

In ancient times ordinary people rarely ate meat. Animals were too valuable as providers of milk, wool or transport to be killed except on very rare occasions. Slaughter, when it happened, was a religious act (i.e. a sacrifice) and an occasion of high rejoicing or great solemnity. Regularly to eat young animals, *lambs from the flock* and *fatted calves*, was the height of profligacy.

5. Amos does not like the contemporary fashion in music (cp. 5: 23). The word translated *pluck the strings* is of doubtful significance. It may be a disapproving description of the sounds made by the singers. We might then translate, 'who wail to the accompaniment of the lute'.

6. Anointing with oil was a sign of festivity. The whole body was rubbed with it, but especially the face. Amos is not opposed to the practice as such, but is shocked by the costliness of the oils used.

Amos is no doubt right to be indignant at the behaviour of Samaria's wealthy socialites, but his apparent assumption that God's taste in furniture, music and cosmetics is the same as his own is open to challenge. The puritan, even at his best, finds it difficult to accept any change of fashion simply as a change of fashion. He has to make a moral issue of it. ✻

THE BLACK DEATH

8 The Lord GOD has sworn by himself:[a]

  I loathe the arrogance of Jacob,
    I loathe his palaces;
  city and all in it I will abandon to their fate.

9 If ten men are left in one house,
    they shall die,

10 and a man's uncle and the embalmer shall take him up
    to carry his body out of the house for burial,
  and they shall call to someone in a corner of the house,
  'Any more there?', and he shall answer, 'No.'
    Then he will add, 'Hush!' –
  for the name of the LORD must not be mentioned.

[a] *So Sept.; Heb. adds* This is the very word of the LORD the God of Hosts.

> For the LORD will command, 11
> and at the shock the great house will be rubble
> and the cottage matchwood.

* Verse 8 is a judgement oracle which follows naturally on the picture of Samaria's decadence, and one can see why the compiler placed it just here, but it has its own separate heading and originally must have begun a new unit. It may well be part and parcel of the description of the plague in verses 9–10. The description is graphic, in spite of some obscurities. The verb translated *I will abandon* in verse 8 can also mean, 'I will shut up', 'enclose', 'imprison'. This is exactly what would happen to a plague-stricken city. It would be isolated and ostracized until the plague had burnt itself out.

10. *the embalmer*, or, alternatively, 'the burner'. Bodies were not normally burnt in Israel, but if the description is correctly interpreted as referring to a plague then the burning of bodies might well be in order. *'Hush!' – for the name of the LORD must not be mentioned.* The plague was thought to be brought on by the Lord, or, more frequently, by his angel; i.e. by a personal, conscious presence. 'Hush!' signifies the super-stitious dread of provoking this presence further, or of drawing attention to any victims which it might have overlooked.

Verse 11 introduces ideas quite foreign to the plague theme. Here the destroyer seems to be an earthquake. This verse should be regarded, therefore, as an independent oracle. *For the LORD will command* is a separate formula of introduction. *

PARADOXES

> Can horses gallop over rocks? 12
> Can the sea be ploughed with oxen?
> Yet you have turned into venom the process of law
> and justice itself into poison,

13   you who are jubilant over a nothing[a] and boast,
    'Have we not won power[a] by our own strength?'
14   O Israel, I am raising a nation against you,
        and they shall harry your land
    from Lebo-hamath to the gorge of the Arabah.
    This is the very word of the LORD the God of Hosts.

✶ This is another two-part oracle. Verses 12–13 are the accusation, of a sort by now familiar, and verse 14 the sentence, that Israel will be conquered by *a nation*. See the note on 5: 27 for this reluctance of Amos to specify the attacker.

13. *Lo-debar* and *Karnaim* (see the N.E.B. note) are cities in the northern Transjordan. They had probably been recently recaptured from the Aramaeans (Syrians). They were not in themselves important towns, but are picked out by the prophet for the sake of the word-play *Lo-debar*, 'No-thing', and *Karnaim*, literally, 'horns'.

14. *Lebo-hamath* is the pass between Lebanon and Anti-Lebanon, the northern limit of Israelite territory. The *Arabah* is the deep valley in which the Dead Sea lies. Where *the gorge of the Arabah* was is uncertain. It was presumably a wadi which in Amos' time was taken as the southern boundary of the kingdom. ✶

Visions foretelling doom upon Israel

We now begin a series of visions, five in all. They consist of two pairs and an odd one. The first two (7: 1–6) are closely similar both in their form and content. In them Amos has

[a] a nothing *and* power: *Heb.* Lo-debar *and* Karnaim, *making a word-play on the two place-names.*

a preview of coming disasters, a locust plague and a 'fire',
which never materialize because he intercedes successfully for
the people.

The second two (7: 7–9, 8: 1–3) are also closely related to
each other, but they are distinct from the first two. What the
prophet 'sees' this time is not the coming disaster itself, but
a symbol of it. The meaning of the symbol is disclosed to him
by God. And this disaster is one which cannot be turned
away by prophetic intercession. It is bound to come.

The fifth vision (9: 1–4) is quite distinct and final. In it the
prophet sees the figure of God himself, intervening in judgement.

The first four visions certainly belong together, and it is
difficult not to imagine Amos recounting all four on the same
occasion. They possess a cumulative force. The first two relate
to a state of affairs now past, in which there was still some hope
of repentance. The second two illustrate the present situation.
There is no longer any hope. God has written Israel off.

The occasion of the fifth vision may have been a different
one, but those who remembered Amos' words remembered
it along with the group of four. When the Amos traditions
were put into written form the series of five visions was
broken up by inserting an account of the Amaziah incident
(7: 10–17) between visions three and four, and interspersing
more detailed condemnations and threats (8: 4–14) between
visions four and five.

Some interpreters connect the visions with Amos' call to
be a prophet, but there is no strong reason for doing this.

THE FIRST PAIR OF VISIONS

THIS WAS WHAT THE LORD GOD showed me: a 7
swarm of locusts hatched out when the late corn,
which comes after the king's early crop, was beginning to
sprout. As they were devouring the last of the herbage in 2

the land, I said, 'O Lord GOD, forgive; what will Jacob
3 be after this? He is so small.' Then the LORD relented
and said, 'This shall not happen.'

4 This was what the Lord GOD showed me: the Lord
GOD was summoning a flame of fire^a to devour the great
5 abyss, and to devour all creation. I said, 'O Lord GOD,
I pray thee, cease; what will Jacob be after this? He is so
6 small.' The LORD relented and said, 'This also shall not
happen.'

✷ 1. *This was what the Lord GOD showed me.* Amos 'sees'
the locusts only in his mind's eye. They are a threat, not an
actuality. The note about the time of year, *when the late corn…*
was beginning to sprout, indicates that Amos is recounting an
experience which took place some months previously. He is
probably speaking later in the same year.

The late corn, which comes after the king's early crop: this
cannot refer to two crops on the same land, for the climate of
Palestine does not allow this. Most probably it does not refer
to *corn* at all (the word 'corn' does not appear in the Hebrew),
but to grass. Two cuts of grass are feasible. The implication
would then be that the king was entitled to the first cut of
grass, presumably for the royal horses. The custom is not,
however, mentioned elsewhere. Some translators, instead of
the king's early crop, render 'the king's shearings', i.e. of sheep.

2. *O Lord GOD, forgive:* God is universally accessible. Anyone can pray to him. Nevertheless, prophets have a special
duty to intercede. Intercession is as much a part of the prophetic office as prediction. In this instance the prophet can
point to no evidence of repentance. He can only appeal to
God's pity.

4. The *flame of fire* in this second vision is often taken as a
metaphor for a severe drought, as in Joel 1: 19. But the use

[a] a flame of fire: *prob. rdg.; Heb.* to contend with fire.

of the fire image in the execration speech (1: 2–2: 16) shows
that it is not for Amos a naturalistic one. This is the supernatural fire of the Lord's judgement. *the great abyss* is the underworld of waters over which the earth stands, according to
ancient near eastern mythology. *

THE THIRD VISION

This was what the LORD showed[a] me: there was a man[b] 7
standing by a wall[c] with a plumb-line in his hand. The 8
LORD said to me, 'What do you see, Amos?' 'A plumb-
line', I answered, and the Lord said, 'I am setting a
plumb-line to the heart of my people Israel; never again
will I pass them by. The hill-shrines of Isaac shall be deso- 9
lated and the sanctuaries of Israel laid waste; I will rise,
sword in hand, against the house of Jeroboam.'

* The point comes when the prophet is forbidden to intercede more. God has made up his mind. Cp. Jer. 11:14. This
vision and the next are of a pattern found elsewhere in prophecy, e.g. Jer. 1: 11–13. The prophet sees an ordinary, mundane object, but it strikes him with peculiar force. It contains
a message. God, or in later prophecy an angel, reveals in dia-
logue with the prophet what this message is. Cp. the visions
in Zech. 1–6.

8. What Amos sees in the third vision is a *plumb-line*. It is
usually said that its purpose is to test whether the wall (Israel)
is straight and true, but there is evidence to suggest that
stretching a measure or weighted line over something was
symbolic of destruction. See, e.g., Lam. 2: 8. *pass them by*
means 'overlook their offences'.

9. The vision leads up to an oracle, and it is this oracle

[a] the LORD showed: *so Sept.; Heb.* he showed.
[b] *So Sept.; Heb.* the Lord.
[c] *Prob. rdg.; Heb. adds* of a plumb-line.

which has prompted the compiler to insert his account of the Amaziah incident at just this point. For the oracle is precisely the sort of statement to which Amaziah was taking exception.

When Amos announces the destruction of *hill-shrines* and *sanctuaries* he is not condemning the multiplicity of places of worship. The multiplicity of sanctuaries was not regarded as undesirable until the Deuteronomists condemned it towards the end of the seventh century ✳

BY WHAT AUTHORITY?

10 Amaziah, the priest of Bethel, reported to Jeroboam king of Israel: 'Amos is conspiring against you in Israel;
11 the country cannot tolerate what he is saying. He says, "Jeroboam shall die by the sword, and Israel shall be
12 deported far from their native land."' To Amos himself Amaziah said, 'Be off, you seer! Off with you to Judah! You can earn your living and do your prophesying there.
13 But never prophesy again at Bethel, for this is the king's
14 sanctuary, a royal palace.' 'I am*a* no prophet,' Amos replied to Amaziah, 'nor am I a prophet's son; I am*a* a
15 herdsman and a dresser*b* of sycomore-figs. But the LORD took me as I followed the flock and said to me, "Go and
16 prophesy to my people Israel." So now listen to the word of the LORD. You tell me I am not to prophesy against Israel or go drivelling on against the people of
17 Isaac. Now these are the words of the LORD: Your wife shall become a city strumpet*c* and your sons and daughters shall fall by the sword. Your land shall be divided up with a measuring-line, you yourself shall die in a heathen

[a] Or was.
[b] *Lit.* pricker.
[c] become...strumpet: *or* be carried off as a prostitute in a raid.

country, and Israel shall be deported far from their native land and go into exile.'

✻ 10. *Amos is conspiring...* looks like a gross misrepresentation, but in Amaziah's terms it is not. Amos has prophesied against the king ('I will rise, sword in hand, against the house of Jeroboam', verse 9). To Amos this is an announcement of divine judgement, but to Amaziah it is sedition. The religious radical threatens the established order, which is why he is often accused of political mischief-making and finds the state and established religion in league against him.

the country cannot tolerate what he is saying: literally, 'cannot contain all his words'. This is more than just a picturesque image. The men of the Old Testament thought of the 'word', especially God's word, as something almost tangible, and certainly as something potent. To prophesy against someone was not merely to utter idle predictions, which could be ignored. The prophetic word was an active force, working to bring about that which it predicted (cp. Isa. 55: 9–11).

11. *Israel shall be deported:* deportation was a characteristic Assyrian policy, but Amos once more does not mention Assyria by name (see note on 5: 27).

12. It is sometimes suggested that *seer* is meant to be derogatory. More likely, however, it is just a synonym for 'prophet' (cp. 1 Sam. 9: 10). Amos takes it so in his reply.

13. *never prophesy again at Bethel, for this is the king's sanctuary:* Bethel was a very ancient shrine, reputed to have been founded by Jacob (Gen. 28: 10–19). After the division of the Kingdom, Jeroboam I tried to establish it as a rival to Jerusalem and it became the principal sanctuary of the Northern Kingdom. It seems that royal sanctuaries were regularly established at or near the borders of the kingdoms, and as well as being very ancient, Bethel was such a border town, being strategically placed on the north–south spinal road and the last northern town of any size before Jerusalem.

14. *prophet's son* is not meant literally. The 'sons of the

prophets' were the prophetic guilds or unions. Amaziah, by saying '*earn your living and do your prophesying there*' (in Judah), has implied that Amos is a professional, and this is what Amos is denying. In saying '*I am no prophet*' Amos does not deny that he carries out prophetic functions. Not only does he regularly use prophetic forms of speech, and fulfil the prophetic office of intercessor (7: 1–6), but in this very passage he protests that he has a call from God to *Go and prophesy* (verse 15). Moreover, his words do not imply any contempt for prophecy's professional exponents; i.e. he is not dissociating himself from the professionals because he despises them. In 2: 11 he cites prophecy as one of God's gifts to Israel.

Amos asserts that professionally he is *a herdsman and a dresser of sycomore-figs*. He is therefore not financially dependent on his prophesying. His intention is to deny that Amaziah has any authority over him, or any right to send him away. The N.E.B. footnote, 'I *was* no prophet', turns the statement into a different kind of justification. If this is the correct rendering, Amos is saying: 'I am not a prophet by training or by my own choice. I was a herdsman, but I received a divine command to be a prophet.' The doubt about the tense arises because in the Hebrew the verb is not expressed, but left to be understood. A fairly literal translation would be, 'No prophet I, nor prophet's son.'

The word translated *herdsman* is a rare one. A similar word turns up in Canaanite texts where it seems to refer to some kind of functionary on the staff of a temple, and some scholars have argued that it might mean the same here. This is extremely improbable. The *sycomore-figs* are actually a species of mulberry, not of high quality as food, and eaten only by the poorest people. They have to be encouraged to ripen by pinching or bruising (cp. the N.E.B.'s note).

15. But if Amos is not a professional, what business has he to be prophesying at all? Has he not himself called his status in question? Amos forestalls this objection by referring to his call from God. *The LORD took me.* He does not exactly

describe this call. What he says amounts to little more than the claim that he did have one. The man of God will rarely refer to his own religious experience. He has to have a strong reason for doing so. Most frequently he resorts to it when his authority is questioned (cp. 2 Cor. 12). It is not only Amaziah who has no control over the prophet's tongue. The prophet himself is not his own master. When the Lord says, 'Go and prophesy', he leaves a man with no option (cp. 3: 8). Compare similar statements by the gentile prophet Balaam (Num. 22:38), by Jeremiah (20: 9) and by the apostles (Acts 4: 19–20).

16–17. Amos turns on Amaziah himself. The tendency of the prophets to answer criticism by cursing the critic is not their most endearing characteristic. But the controlling idea here is that criticism of the prophet's word is not so much a personal attack on the prophet as an act of sacrilege (cp. Jer. 28: 15–17). Amaziah, who is a priest and ought to know better, has suggested that a prophet should refrain from speaking what God has given him to speak.

And Israel shall be deported: Amos repeats the words complained of. A prophecy which has been challenged must be reasserted if it is to preserve its force. Cp. Jer. 36: 27–32.

We do not know what the sequel to these events was. The likeliest outcome is that Amos left, under protest, for Judah. ✻

THE FOURTH VISION

This was what the Lord GOD showed me: there was a **8** basket of summer fruit, and he said, 'What are you look- 2 ing at, Amos?' I answered, 'A basket of ripe summer[a] fruit.' Then the LORD said to me, 'The time is ripe[a] for my people Israel. Never again will I pass them by. In that day, 3 says the Lord GOD, the singing women in the palace shall

[a] ripe summer *and* ripe: *a play on the Heb.* qais (summer) *and* qes (end).

howl, "So many dead men, flung out everywhere! Silence!"'

✱ 1. If the *basket of summer fruit* was an actual object which the prophet happened to see, this would fix the time of year as autumn. The 'summer fruits', grapes, figs, olives, etc., appear from late August or early September onwards. The message which the vision contains turns on a similarity of words, a pun (see the N.E.B. note). This to us suggests a trivial connection, and we should find it hard to take seriously a prophetic message arrived at in this fashion. No man of ancient times would have looked at it in that way, however. To him, a similarity between the names of things involved a real relationship between the things themselves. Simply because its name (*qais*) recalls a more ominous word (*qes* – 'end'), Amos can take a familiar object of the autumn harvest festival and turn this innocent and cheerful thing into a portent of doom.

Verse 3 is an oracle appended to the vision, as the oracle of 7: 9 is appended to the vision of the plumb-line. It is on several counts difficult to translate, and translators vary in their solutions to the problem. Its disjointed end may be due to textual corruption, or it may be the abrupt, enigmatic utterance of the ecstatic. Amos seems to specialize in these fragmentary pictures, whose very lack of clarity makes them the more menacing, like snatches of bad dreams. ✱

INTERLUDE

After these four visions there is an interlude before the fifth and final one. Verses 4–7 again expatiate on the economic and social sins of Israel, and there are three interposed sections anticipating what is to happen *on that day*, i.e. on the imminent day of retribution. These probably comprise a small independent collection of oracles. The compiler here has worked with conscious artistry, skilfully delaying his climax, the final vision, which is of the day of judgement itself.

Listen to this, you who grind the destitute and plunder[a] 4
the humble, you who say, 'When will the new moon be 5
over so that we may sell corn? When will the sabbath be
past so that we may open our wheat again, giving short
measure in the bushel[b] and taking overweight in the
silver, tilting the scales fraudulently, and selling the dust 6
of the wheat; that we may buy the poor for silver and
the destitute for a pair of shoes?' The LORD has sworn 7
by the pride of Jacob: I will never forget any of their
doings.

✻ 5. *new moon...sabbath:* the two are often mentioned together in pre-exilic texts as though they were parallel and
comparable festal days. We have no guarantee that the sabbath
at this period took the form which is so familiar to us from
later times. However, it is clear from what Amos says that
both it and the new moon were days when buying and selling
were forbidden or restricted.

The offences complained of are against the poor and defenceless. Amos is not criticizing the merchants for sabbath-
breaking. They do, in fact, keep the sabbath, in spite of their
impatience. *bushel,* literally 'ephah', a measure of about ten
gallons (forty litres). *taking overweight in the silver:* coinage
was still unknown. Money had to be weighed out for each
transaction. Standardization of weights was difficult to achieve
in ancient societies, and to use non-standard ones a very easy
way of defrauding the customer.

6. The last part of this verse, *that we may buy...,* is repeated
here, in error, from 2: 6.

7. When Amos reports that *the LORD has sworn by the
pride of Jacob,* his intention is ironic. One swears by what
is fixed and unalterable, hence 'by Jacob's monumental
pride'. ✻

[a] and plunder: *prob. rdg.; Heb.* to destroy.   [b] *Heb.* ephah.

8   Shall not the earth shake for this?
        Shall not all who live on it grieve?
      All earth shall surge and seethe like the Nile*a*
        and subside like the river of Egypt.

* This verse is obscure, having no apparent logical connection
either with what precedes or with what follows it. It is a
snatch of poetry or hymn, quoted more fully in 9: 5–6, and
possibly out of place here. *

9   On that day, says the Lord GOD,
        I will make the sun go down at noon
        and darken the earth in broad daylight.
10   I will turn your pilgrim-feasts into mourning
        and all your songs into lamentation.
        I will make you all put sackcloth round your waists
        and have all your heads shaved.
        I will make it like mourning for an only son
        and the end of it a bitter day.

11   The time is coming, says the Lord GOD,
        when I will send famine on the land,
      not hunger for bread or thirst for water,
        but for hearing the word of the LORD.
12   Men shall stagger from north to south,*b*
        they shall range from east to west,
      seeking the word of the LORD,
        but they shall not find it.
13   On that day fair maidens and young men
        shall faint from thirst;

        [a] the Nile: *so some MSS., cp. 9: 5; others* the light.
        [b] south: *prob. rdg.; Heb.* west.

all who take their oath by Ashimah, goddess of 14
    Samaria,
all who swear, 'By the life of your god, O Dan',
and, 'By the sacred way to[a] Beersheba',
shall fall to rise no more.

* These three oracles have been placed together because of
their similarity of subject-matter. Oracles 2 and 3 are further
connected by the catchword 'thirst'.

In the first oracle, verses 9–10, the day of retribution is
pictured mainly in cultic terms, though the darkness at noon
adds a non-naturalistic dimension to it. This darkness is a
feature of the stereotyped imagery in which appearances of
God were described. It is pointless to decide that verse 9 refers
to an eclipse and then to try and identify the eclipse.

10. On the turning of a festival of rejoicing into a season of
mourning see the note on 5: 16–17.

The imagery of the second oracle (verses 11–12) is that of
the famine. But this is a figurative famine, *not hunger for bread
or thirst for water, but for hearing the word of the LORD*. This is
the most serious sign of God's rejection of his people. He has
nothing more to say to them. Cp. the notes on Hos. 5: 6.

The third oracle (verses 13–14) takes up the theme of
'thirst', but is prophesying an actual drought, not a metaphorical one. This oracle contains one of Amos' rare references
to religious malpractice. The *Ashimah…of Samaria* is unlikely to have been a substitute for Yahweh, more likely his
female consort. *Dan* was a shrine in the far north, which
Jeroboam I elevated into a national sanctuary along with
Bethel. He placed bull images at both centres, but it is probable
that he intended these bulls to represent the national deity
(but see note on Hos. 8: 5–6). This was decidedly unorthodox
by later standards, but those who, in Amos' time, swore '*By
the life of your god, O Dan*', would not think of themselves as

[a] sacred way to: *or, with Sept.,* life of your god, O…

63

apostates. Neither does swearing '*By the sacred way to Beersheba*' in itself imply apostasy. Beersheba (which is, incidentally, in Judah, not in Israel) was ostensibly a sanctuary of the Lord. The form of this oath may seem curious, but oaths of exactly this type are attested among the Moslem Arabs. There are, however, other possible interpretations. The word rendered 'way' may actually mean 'your pantheon'. The *fair maidens and young men* are the youngest and strongest of the community. When they faint, all have fainted (cp. Isa. 40: 31). *

PREPARE TO MEET YOUR GOD

9   I saw the LORD standing by the altar, and he said:

Strike the capitals so that the whole porch is shaken;
    I will smash them all into pieces*a*
    and I will kill them to the last man*b* with the sword.
    No fugitive shall escape,
    no survivor find safety;
2   if they dig down to Sheol,
    thence shall my hand take them;
        if they climb up to heaven,
        thence will I bring them down.
3   If they hide on the top of Carmel,
        there will I search out and take them;
    if they conceal themselves from me in the depths of the
        sea,
    there will I bid the sea-serpent bite them.
4   If they are herded into captivity by their enemies,
        there will I bid the sword slay them,
        and I will fix my eye on them
        for evil and not for good.

[a] I will...pieces: *prob. rdg.; Heb.* I will hack them on the heads of them all.   [b] them to the last man: *or* their children.

✻ Amos, probably speaking at the Autumn Festival, antici-pates the festival's climax, the appearance of God in the sanctuary. And this brings us also to the climax of the book.

Those who desire the appearance of the Lord may not find the encounter quite what they expect. Let the religious man beware. The living God may at any time break through the rituals and the ceremonies and make them mean what they say. In contrast with the previous visions, what Amos sees this time is not the mere threat of catastrophe, nor symbols of it, but the Lord himself.

1. *I saw the LORD standing*...: such a claim is not unique in prophecy. Its closest parallels are Isa. 6: 1 and 1 Kings 22: 19. Both Isaiah and Micaiah report, 'I saw the Lord, seated...' The difference in posture is significant. In Israel a king sits in council, but he stands when he delivers judgement.

The very word 'sanctuary' speaks of security and safety. God's presence there, in their midst, was the basis of the people's confidence. It is at this very point that God begins his destructive work. Amos agrees that God will manifest himself in the sanctuary. But he will not preside in blessing, he will erupt in judgement. He will shatter the columns on the heads of the congregation and exterminate them *to the last man*. About a century earlier Jehu had trapped the worshippers of Baal inside a sanctuary and slaughtered them all. Is Amos thinking of this incident (2 Kings 10: 18-28)?

The imagery has again suggested to some that Amos is thinking of an earthquake as the means of destruction, but it is unlikely that he intends to be so specific. Amos is not con-cerned with the machinery of judgement, but with the fact of it. It is perhaps equally academic to ask whom God is address-ing when he says '*Strike the capitals*...'. Possibly he is address-ing unnamed agents, human or superhuman, but more likely he is speaking to no-one at all. The divine decree is self-implementing. It only needs to be uttered in order to be fulfilled.

The pursuit of the would-be survivors is described in terms

strongly recalling Psalm 139. The psalm expresses the idea that the devotee is nowhere beyond the reach of God's power. For the psalmist this is a reason for profound confidence. Amos again is taking the language of comfort and turning it into a threat.

2. *if they dig down to Sheol...*: i.e. the underworld.

3. *Carmel* is mentioned as a hiding place probably because it is riddled with caves and heavily wooded. The *sea-serpent* is the mythical Leviathan, the chaos-monster in person.

4. The final reference to *captivity* is the most damning threat of all. Up to now the prophet has represented captivity, i.e. deportation, as the worst fate God can impose on the nation. But even that is not severe enough, for the captive has hope, however slender, of return. And for Israel there is now no hope at all. ⁕

5   The Lord the GOD of Hosts,
          at whose touch the earth heaves,
             and all who dwell on it wither,[a]
          it surges like the Nile,
             and subsides like the river of Egypt,
6   who builds his stair up to[b] the heavens
          and arches his ceiling over the earth,
             who summons the waters of the sea
          and pours them over the land –
             his name is the LORD.

⁕ This is the last of the short, hymn-like passages described in the note on 4: 13. It interrupts the flow of thought, for verses 7–8 *a* clearly continue the thought of verse 4.

5. *at whose touch the earth heaves*: the N.E.B.'s translation here turns the whole verse into a description of an earthquake.

[a] Or mourn.
[b] stair up to: or, *with slight change*, upper chambers in.

Amos may not have meant to be so definite. 'The earth melts' would be a more literal rendering. God's 'touching the earth' could be intended to refer to storm, lightning, drought or any of a dozen other natural phenomena.

6. *and pours them* (the waters) *over the land:* i.e. in the violent winter storms, which in Palestine frequently do serious damage. ✻

> Are not you Israelites like Cushites to me?
>> says the LORD.   7
> Did I not bring Israel up from Egypt,
> the Philistines from Caphtor, the Aramaeans from Kir?
>> Behold, I, the Lord GOD,
>> have my eyes on this sinful kingdom,   8*a*
> and I will wipe it off the face of the earth.

✻ These verses deny that Israel has any privileged position before God, and thus formally contradict the statement in 3: 2, 'For you alone have I cared among all the nations of the world.' In 3: 2 Amos is saying that the special relationship between God and Israel carries special responsibilities rather than privileges. Here, in an effort to refute the idea that Israel has any claim to lenient treatment, he goes so far as to deny that the special relationship exists at all. He does not deny that God was responsible for the exodus. He simply puts the exodus on the same footing as the migrations of other peoples. Cp. Deut. 2: 5 and 2: 9, but contrast Judg. 11: 24.

7. *Cushites* means Ethiopians, selected for mention because they are remote and strange. *Caphtor* is probably Crete, and to connect the Philistines with Crete is more or less accurate. They probably came from the Aegean coastlands, entering Palestine only a little later than Israel's own invasion. The *Aramaeans* (Syrians) came from further east. They settled at about the same period as the Philistines, but in the region of Syria, developing from pastoral semi-nomads into an urban society much as Israel did, but somewhat more slowly.   ✻

A remnant spared and restored

THE HAPPY ENDING

8*b*   Yet I will not wipe out the family of Jacob root and
branch,
    says the LORD.

9   No; I will give my orders,
I will shake Israel to and fro through all the nations
    as a sieve is shaken to and fro
    and not one pebble falls to the ground.

10   They shall die by the sword, all the sinners of my
people,
    who say, 'Thou wilt not let disaster come near us
    or overtake us.'

11   On that day I will restore
    David's fallen house;*a*
I will repair its*b* gaping walls and restore its*c* ruins;
    I will rebuild it as it was long ago,

12   that they may possess what is left of Edom
and all the nations who were once named mine.

This is the very word of the LORD, who will do this.

13   A time is coming, says the LORD,
    when the ploughman shall follow hard on the
        vintager,*d*
and he who treads the grapes after him who sows the
    seed.

[a] *Lit.* booth.   [b] *So Sept.; Heb.* their.
[c] *So Sept.; Heb.* his.   [d] *Or* reaper.

The mountains shall run with fresh wine,
and every hill shall wave with corn.

I will restore the fortunes of my people Israel;   14
they shall rebuild deserted cities and live in them,
they shall plant vineyards and drink their wine,
make gardens and eat the fruit.

Once more I will plant them on their own soil,   15
and they shall never again be uprooted
from the soil I have given them.
It is the word of the LORD your God.

* Apart from these last verses there is no optimistic prophecy
in Amos, and most of these verses are manifestly later additions. Why this lack of cheerful predictions? Virtually all
other prophets seem to have uttered salvation oracles sometimes. Why are no authentic ones recorded of Amos? The
simplest, and still the likeliest, explanation is that Amos
genuinely sees no future for the nation. The judgement is
final. Nevertheless, two other explanations are at least possible.

(1) Amos is preoccupied with the great, the exemplary
punishment of Israel's sins. His message of destruction so ob-
sesses him that he cannot or will not look beyond it to the
question of what happens afterwards. Whether beyond the
judgement the mercy of God might again operate is not for
him to ask. Even to contemplate that there might *be* an
'afterwards' would be to deprive his message of its radical
nature and his threat of its full potency.

(2) Another possibility is that Amos did, on occasion, utter
prophecies of salvation, but they were suppressed. Amos was
speaking originally about the Northern Kingdom. Now those
who first collected Amos' oracles knew that in fact Israel did
not survive the destruction of 722 B.C. She never regained her
independence, and did not preserve even her national identity.
There might at this stage have been a strong temptation to

make the prophecies correspond more closely to events, not by adding words of comfort, but by suppressing any which the prophet may have spoken.

At a later stage, during the exile or after, the prophecies were edited by southerners. By then the Northern Kingdom had been long defunct, and the editors instinctively read the prophecies as a message to Judah, and as a comfort to its Judaean readers the book was made to finish with a promise.

Verses 8*b*–10 cannot in their present state have been spoken by Amos, but at the core of this oracle there may be a genuine word of his. The image of the sieve, as it now stands, suggests a selective judgement; only *the sinners of my people* shall *die by the sword*. But if the prophet himself spoke of this shaking of the nation he may have meant something more uncompromising.

Verses 11–12 are possibly a separate unit.

11. *David's fallen house* is the Davidic dynasty, and these words presuppose that it had come to an end. They must therefore have been written later than the fall of Jerusalem in 586 B.C. The sentiments expressed here would fit excellently into the period of Zerubbabel.

12. *Edom:* see commentary on 1: 11–12.

The beautiful salvation oracle of verses 13–15 is a separate unit. The point of the imagery is that the harvests will be so abundant that men will not have finished gathering them before it is time for the next round of agricultural operations. The theme of an age to come in which the land will be miraculously fertile is common in apocalyptic literature, but there it is usually developed more fancifully than here. This oracle therefore comes from the earlier, more restrained phase of eschatological expectations.

14. *they shall rebuild deserted cities and live in them, they shall plant vineyards and drink their wine, make gardens and eat the fruit:* whoever added these words was careful to annul the dreadful curse of 5: 11. ✳

✳   ✳   ✳   ✳   ✳   ✳   ✳   ✳   ✳   ✳   ✳   ✳   ✳

HOSEA

✻ ✻ ✻ ✻ ✻ ✻ ✻ ✻ ✻ ✻ ✻ ✻ ✻

THE RELIGION OF ISRAEL
AND THE RELIGION OF CANAAN

Before Hosea can be understood we must understand something of the conflict of religions which was taking place in Palestine in his day. Before Israel conquered Palestine the land was inhabited by people whom we may broadly call 'Canaanites'. They had a religion of their own which was very rich and diverse in its myths, ideas and rites. There is no space here for a full account of Canaanite religion, but a knowledge of some features of it is vital to an understanding of Hosea.

The Canaanites worshipped a pantheon of gods. The most important in practice, though not in theory the chief god, was Baal. Baal was the god of rain and the giver of fertility. His enemy was Moth, the god of summer drought and of death. According to the Canaanite myths Baal fought with Moth and was defeated and killed. His death was avenged by the goddess Anath and he appears to have risen from the dead.

Baal is spoken of as the husband of the land, and his relations with the land and with his people are spoken of in sexual terms. The worship of Baal evidently involved sacred prostitution; that is, prostitutes were kept on the staff of the sanctuary, and men indulged in sexual intercourse with them as an act of worship. This act was supposed to help ensure fertility by repeating, sacramentally, the god's marriage with the land. The profession of such prostitutes was thought of as holy, not degrading.

The religion which Israel brought with her into Palestine was very different. Her God, Yahweh, was originally a God

The book of Hosea

of the desert, whose chief claim on Israel was that he had saved her from bondage in Egypt. (On the contrast between the two gods, see further on p. 84.)

When Israel conquered Palestine she did not eliminate the existing population. She settled among them, and eventually the Israelite and Canaanite stocks were assimilated. This assimilation of the population was probably complete by the time of Solomon. The two *religions*, however, remained in conflict for some time longer.

From the time of the conquest itself two tendencies were apparent:

(1) Whereas most Israelites would doubtless have regarded Yahweh as the national God, it was tempting to assume that Baal was the provider of the good things of the land and to worship him in order to make sure of the land's continued fertility. (A desert God would manifestly have had little experience in this sphere.) Thus it seems that, in the early years of settlement, many Israelites became Baal-worshippers in practice though they regarded themselves as entitled to call on the old warrior Yahweh in times of crisis. This amounted to preserving the two religions side by side.

(2) Later, however, the tendency was to blur the distinction between the two faiths, to combine the functions of the rival deities and to take over the rites of the one religion into the other.

Those, like the canonical prophets, who championed Israel's old national faith, could adopt two alternative positions. They could insist rigidly on the distinction between the two religions and try to keep Yahwism as close as possible to its ancient form. (This is likely to have been Amos' position.) Or they could, up to a point, encourage the broadening of the national faith. They could assert that Yahweh really had taken over the functions of Baal; that he was responsible for the fertility of the land; that it was he, and not Baal, 'who gave (Israel) corn, new wine, and oil' (Hos. 2: 8). But those who were thus ready to take over ideas from Baalism had to be especially careful to insist that this must not involve taking over degrading rites and forms of worship.

Hosea is adopting this latter course, for in his day the struggle with Baal-worship was by no means over. He is bitterly opposed to Baalism, but he takes over its own imagery and language as weapons with which to fight it. He also seems to have learnt something from it. The Baal-worshippers were well acquainted with the idea that God is love, although they were inclined to interpret this as meaning that God is sex. Hosea rejects this interpretation of the matter, but in the Baalist idea of the God who yearns for his people and who never casts them off he finds something irresistible. To combine this with his own tradition of the demanding God of covenant is in some ways easy, but in others very difficult, and the tension between the old tradition and the new insight is felt throughout the book.

* * * * * * * * * * * * *

THE TITLE

THE WORD OF THE LORD which came to Hosea son 1 of Beeri during the reigns of Uzziah, Jotham, Ahaz, and Hezekiah, kings of Judah, and during the reign of Jeroboam son of Jehoash king of Israel.

* 1. This is the heading of the entire book, added by an editor after the material had been brought south. The editor seems to have had only a rough idea of the date of Hosea's activities. Of the northern kings the only one mentioned is Jeroboam II, though it is certain that Hosea did much of his prophesying after the end of Jeroboam's reign (see p. 3). We are given no personal details about Hosea except his father's name. We do not know his occupation and are given no explicit information about his place of origin. It is generally assumed that he was a northerner.

Hosea's unfaithful wife

THE MARRIAGE THEME IN HOSEA

Chapters 1–3 of Hosea are a collection of pieces bearing on the same theme. The theme is a double one, of the prophet's relations with his wife and God's relations with Israel. Hosea has used the facts about his own married life in order to convey God's word. Neither he nor his compiler was interested in biographical detail for its own sake. As a result, much that we should like to know is left unsaid.

These chapters are not a consistent and orderly exposition of the subject. They are a collection of materials which happen to be related to the same theme but, having been spoken on different occasions, treat it in different ways. We thus get an impression of violent oscillation between opposite poles of thinking and feeling. The prophet's own relations with his wife and God's relations with Israel are so intertwined that we cannot always be sure at any given moment which of them is uppermost in his mind. The feelings expressed alternate between disillusionment and hope, between tenderness and outrage. And the treatment he proposes for the offender varies between fierce discipline and passionate appeal.

✓ HOSEA'S CHILDREN

2 THIS IS THE BEGINNING of the LORD's message by Hosea. He said, Go, take a wanton for your wife and get children of her wantonness; for like a wanton this land 3 is unfaithful to the LORD. So he went and took Gomer, a worthless woman;[a] and she conceived and bore him a son. 4 And the LORD said to him,

[a] a worthless woman: *or* daughter of Diblaim.

Call him Jezreel;[a] for in a little while
I will punish the line of Jehu for the blood shed in
      Jezreel
  and put an end to the kingdom of Israel.
    On that day   5
I will break Israel's bow in the Vale of Jezreel.

She conceived again and bore a daughter, and the LORD 6
said to him,

  Call her Lo-ruhamah;[b]
for I will never again show love to Israel,
  never again forgive them.[c]

After weaning Lo-ruhamah, she conceived and bore a son; 8
and the LORD said,   9

  Call him Lo-ammi;[d]
    for you are not my people,
  and I will not be your God.[e]

✻ These verses tell how the prophet married a *wanton* woman
and how he named the children of the marriage. Chapter 3
tells of his relations with a woman of similar character; how he
acquired her, by buying her or buying her back; and how he
disciplined her. Are these two accounts of the same thing or
of two different things? A whole catalogue of theories is
possible:

[a] *That is* God shall sow.
[b] *That is* Not loved.
[c] *Prob. rdg.; Heb. adds* (7) Then I will love Judah and will save them.
I will save them not by bow or sword or weapon of war, by horses or
by horsemen, but by the LORD their God.
[d] *That is* Not my people.
[e] your God: *lit.* yours.

A. They refer to different events.

(1) They refer to different events and concern different women. Chapter 1 tells of the prophet's marriage; chapter 3 recounts a symbolic action involving a slave woman. Such so-called symbolic actions are not uncommon in prophecy. They are better called enacted prophecies. In such enactments the prophet acts out his message as in a little drama, an enacted parable. Other examples are found, e.g., in Jer. 27–8, Isa. 20.

(2) They refer to different events but the same woman; i.e. they relate successive phases in Hosea's relations with his wife. Even here at least two reconstructions are possible. (*a*) The events of chapter 3 precede those of chapter 1. Hosea takes a woman of known loose morals. He disciplines her and hopes she has reformed. He marries her and has children, but later she is found unfaithful. (*b*) Chapter 1 precedes chapter 3. Hosea marries Gomer in good faith. She is unfaithful to him and he rejects her. But later he buys her back and disciplines her. Those who opt for this interpretation sometimes argue that chapter 3 has been misplaced, and that originally it followed straight on after 1: 9. The N.E.B. translators evidently favour this view, as they indicate in their note to 3: 1.

B. The two accounts, in spite of their differences, are really describing the same happening.

Any view of the relations between the two chapters raises problems. The view taken in this commentary is that we have two accounts of the same event. The chief difficulty for this interpretation is that in 3: 1 the prophet is told, 'Go *again* and love a woman...' This word 'again' was probably inserted by an editor who himself did not appreciate that the two chapters refer to the same happening.

The differences between the two accounts are explained by the fact that they have been put together for quite different purposes. The interest of chapter 1 is primarily in the prophetic names of the children. This account is placed first by the book's

compiler because other oracles refer back to these names and
would be incomprehensible without some explanation of
them. Chapter 3 is concerned mainly with the actual purchase
of the woman (or the payment of the bride-price for her) and
with the conditions laid on her in the marriage contract.

The fact that chapter 3 is in the first person suggests that it
may be the way the prophet himself told the story. The third
person form of chapter 1 suggests that the collector of the
oracles, or some earlier disciple, composed it.

2. The words, *Go, take a wanton for your wife*, seem to imply
that Hosea knew when he married Gomer what kind of
woman she was. Some readers find this incredible. They conclude that he did not know at the time, but that looking back
on it he could see that the experience was the will of God.
That Hosea should believe that God commanded him knowingly to marry a woman of loose morals is certainly repugnant
to our way of thinking, but it is not on that account false.
On the alternative theory Hosea must have believed that
God commanded him *un*knowingly to marry a woman of
loose morals. Is this less objectionable?

The simplest interpretation of Hosea's words is that his
marriage to Gomer was a piece of enacted prophecy. The
direct commands, *Take a wanton for your wife* (1: 2), and
'Love a woman loved by another man, an adulteress' (3: 1),
are the point at which the two chapters most closely agree.
The precise nature of Gomer's sexual errors is not clear.
Whether she was an actual prostitute, as the word *wanton*
suggests, or simply an adulteress, as suggested by 3:1, is
hardly important. The main point is that she was in some
manner sexually promiscuous. It has been suggested that she
was, or had been, a cult prostitute. This is plausible, but we
have no positive evidence that it was so. Whatever the truth
of the matter, we must concede that Hosea became genuinely
involved with the woman emotionally, and that his love for
her was real.

We, of course, know only the prophet's side of the story,

and little enough of that. It is doubtless idle to speculate what it felt like to be married to someone as intense as a Hebrew prophet, or how a girl of spirit might have reacted to the thought of being married off as a bit of somebody else's prophetic symbolism.

4. Hosea is preoccupied with the significance of places and their names, and especially with *Jezreel*, which he keeps coming back to in different connections. Jezreel is the name of his first child, possibly given when he still had hopes that his marriage would turn out well. Its meaning, 'God sows', seems to reflect this hope.

The name Jezreel also recalled a shattering experience for northern prophecy. The northern prophets seem to have taken it on themselves to supervise the monarchy (a notion which the northern kings, for the most part, resented) and on a number of occasions they were instrumental in overthrowing dynasties of which they disapproved. The last occasion on which they did this was when they instigated the bloody revolution of Jehu, which centred on Jezreel. The story is told in 2 Kings 9. Jezreel was the place where Ahab had murdered Naboth, and, appropriately, the prophets are said to have announced it as the place where vengeance would be taken on Ahab's house and Ahab's queen (1 Kings 21). Jehu's reign, however, was a disaster, and Hosea, speaking about a century later, recognizes the revolution to have been a mistake. Jezreel, therefore, will now be the place where *the line of Jehu* itself meets its doom. Hence Jezreel, to Hosea, speaks of the failure of the whole policy of northern prophecy from the time of the division of the Kingdom onwards.

In view of this it would not be surprising if he had seen the secession of the Northern Kingdom itself as a mistake, and looked forward to the reunion of the two halves of the nation. Other prophets certainly did so; though, to be sure, they were all southern prophets. See also the notes on 1: 11.

So far, then, the name Jezreel is connected for the prophet with disillusionment, with the failure of his domestic expectations, and with the failure of the prophetic movement to which he belonged. But in itself the name is an auspicious one, a fact which a prophet could not but have regarded as significant. Jezreel, in spite of its unpleasant associations, speaks of hope. Even at the place of men's failures 'God sows'.

6. *Lo-ruhamah* ('Unloved') may indicate that the prophet does not recognize this second child as his own offspring. Be that as it may, on the national level it signifies the rejection by God of his people. *never again forgive them* can alternatively be translated, 'I will utterly take them away.'

7. This verse, relegated by the N.E.B. to a footnote, is universally admitted to be an addition by a Judaean editor. It insists that the word 'Israel' in the previous verses means the Northern Kingdom only, and exempts Judah from the judgement. Its inclusion may have been prompted by the almost miraculous escape of Jerusalem from Sennacherib's attack at the end of the eighth century.

8. *After weaning Lo-ruhamah* implies an interval of some years. Children were breast-fed up to two or three years old.

9. *Lo-ammi:* see N.E.B. footnote. *you are not my people, and I will not be your God* is a blunt reversal of the terms of the covenant between God and Israel. ✷

THE REUNION OF THE NATION

The Israelites shall become countless as the sands of the 10[a]
    sea
  which can neither be measured nor numbered;
it shall no longer be said, 'They are not my people',
  they shall be called Sons of the Living God.
Then the people of Judah and of Israel shall be reunited 11
  and shall choose for themselves a single head,
    and they shall become masters of the earth;
    for great shall be the day of Jezreel.

[a] 2: 1 *in Heb.*

79

Then you will say to your brothers, 'You are my
people',
and to your sisters, 'You are loved.'

* This is a separate oracle from the preceding one, placed
here because it happens to refer to Lo-ammi, Lo-ruhamah
and Jezreel. Some think it was added by Hosea's disciples after
the fall of the Northern Kingdom. But if we concede that
Hosea might have looked forward to the reunion of all Israel
there is nothing in the oracle that could not be his.

10. The phrase, *shall become countless as the sands of the sea*,
recalls the promise to Abraham in Gen. 22: 16–19. The renewal of the nation's unity renews hope that the ancient
promise might be fulfilled.

The phrase rendered by the N.E.B., *it shall no longer be said*,
reads literally, 'in the place where it was said'. The literal
rendering is better preserved. Hosea's 'place symbolism' has
already been remarked on. He is here saying that the place
of betrayal and rejection is to become the place of restoration
and reconciliation. The reconciliation of the two halves of
the nation will be simultaneous with the reconciliation of
the nation with its God.

What is this place which Hosea is talking about? It might
be Jezreel itself. In verse 11 the day of reconciliation seems to
be called *the day of Jezreel*. But a better candidate is Shechem.
Shechem was the place where Joshua made the covenant with
the tribes after the conquest (Josh. 24) and the place where
Israel rejected the house of David after the accession of
Rehoboam (1 Kings 12) and thus became 'Not my people'.

11. *a single head*: it may be significant that Hosea avoids the
word 'king'. Perhaps he visualized reunion under some form
of government other than the monarchy (see note on 3: 5).
and they shall become masters of the earth: this is a difficult
sentence to translate. An alternative rendering is, 'and they
shall go up from the land', i.e. to Shechem, to take part in
the coronation of the ruler and the renewing of the covenant.

To whom are the words of 2: 1 addressed? The N.E.B.,
keeping to the received Hebrew text, implies that it is the
people who are being spoken to. They are to acknowledge
their fellows of the other half of the nation with the words,
'*You are my people*', '*You are loved*'. God uses the same words
to acknowledge themselves. Unloved Israel becomes loved
when she is prepared to love her neighbour. Some prefer to
see the words as addressed to Hosea's son, Jezreel, but this
involves altering the text to read, 'Then you will say to your
brother...and to your *sister*...' ✳

THREATS AGAINST THE WANTON

Plead my cause with your mother;   2
is she not my wife and I her husband?[a]
Plead with her to forswear those wanton looks,
to banish the lovers from her bosom.
Or I will strip her and expose her   3
naked as the day she was born;
I will make her bare as the wilderness,
parched as the desert,
and leave her to die of thirst.
I will show no love for her children;   4
they are the offspring of wantonness,
and their mother is a wanton.   5
She who conceived them is shameless;
she says, 'I will go after my lovers;
they give me my food and drink,
my wool and flax, my oil and my perfumes.'
Therefore I will block her[b] road with thorn-bushes   6
and obstruct her path[c] with a wall,

[a] is she...husband?: *or* for she is no longer my wife nor I her husband.
[b] *So Sept.; Heb.* your.
[c] *Prob. rdg., cp. Sept.; Heb.* her wall.

so that she can no longer follow her old ways.

7   When she pursues her lovers she will not overtake
        them,
        when she looks for them she will not find them;
          then she will say,
    'I will go back to my husband again;
      I was better off with him than I am now.'

8   For she does not know that it is I who gave her
      corn, new wine, and oil,
      I who lavished upon her silver and gold
        which they spent on the Baal.

9   Therefore I will take back
my corn at the harvest and my new wine at the
            vintage,
      and I will take away the wool and the flax
        which I gave her to cover her naked body;

10   so I will show her up for the lewd thing she is,
and no lover will want to steal her from me.

12*a* I will ravage the vines and the fig-trees,
      which she says are the fee
      with which her lovers have hired her,
and turn them into jungle where wild beasts shall feed.

11   I will put a stop to her merrymaking,
her pilgrimages and new moons, her sabbaths*b* and
            festivals.

13   I will punish her for the holy days
      when she burnt sacrifices to the Baalim,
      when she decked herself with earrings and necklaces,
ran after her lovers and forgot me.
      This is the very word of the LORD.

[*a*] *Verses 11 and 12 transposed.*   [*b*] *Or* her full moons.

✻ Here we have a collection of poems or fragments of poems put together because of the similar imagery which they use. At least three original pieces can be picked out. Verses 2-5 and 8-9 come from a single speech threatening the adulteress with divorce and disgrace. Verses 6-7 are an inserted snatch of material whose background is lost. The image of the unfaithful wife is treated rather differently in it. The talk about chasing lovers and being restrained by hedges and walls is more appropriate to an animal on heat than to a human being (cp. Jer. 2: 23-4). Verses 11-13 (12, 11, 13 in the N.E.B.'s order) are included at this point because of their mention of adultery. But the mention is a passing one. The main point of the verses is a condemnation of the cult.

In the principal section, verses 2-5 and 8-9, the prophet is thinking simultaneously of his unfaithful wife and the unfaithful Israel, and his language is appropriate sometimes to the one, sometimes to the other. It has been suggested that this speech is modelled on the established legal procedure for the prosecution of adulterous wives. The accusation is made and punishment is then called for. This interpretation demands a rendering of verse 2 in accordance with the N.E.B. footnote. Thus translated the speech contains a formal declaration that the marriage is at an end.

The difficulty with this suggestion is that the speech seems to be addressed not to a court but to the children. The speech is best taken, therefore, not as a formal legal accusation, but as the threat of one. The prophet reminds his wife of the power which he possesses to punish and humiliate her if he chose to use it. Verse 3 supports this interpretation by making the whole thing conditional. Let her behave herself, says the prophet, *or I will strip her...*

The punishment envisaged seems to consist in stripping the woman naked in public. The laws of the Old Testament allow no such punishment, recognizing only the death penalty as proper for adultery. But Ezek. 16: 35-9 seems to presuppose that it was used, and we know that it was used elsewhere in the ancient Near East.

3. With the words, *I will make her bare as the wilderness, parched as the desert*, the prophet passes readily from the stripping of the woman to the stripping of the land. God will deprive the country of all those things which Israel thought she owed to Baal, the great lover (see above, pp. 72–3). It is sometimes said that Baal was a nature god, whereas Yahweh, the God of Israel, was a God of history, i.e. a saviour God, whose characteristic was that he had delivered Israel from her enemies. This may be broadly true, but the distinction is not absolute. The God who brought the plagues on the Egyptians and dried up the Red Sea must have had control over nature. Baal, for his part, was also in some sense a saviour god. Like Yahweh he was famous for his battles. But Baal's battles are all mythical. He fights the Sea, and he fights Moth (Death), the god of summer drought. Yahweh's battles are mostly historical, against the Egyptians at the time of the exodus, against those who resisted Israel's conquest of the land of Canaan or disputed her possession of it afterwards.

But if there was only one Baal, why speak of Israel's *lovers*, in the plural? It is partly, no doubt, because the plural fits the metaphor of harlotry better, but partly because Baal was worshipped at many shrines and perhaps took on a different character at each. Hence verse 13 can speak of *the Baalim* (the English plural, 'baals', might be better).

11–13. The licentiousness castigated here did not merely accompany Baal worship, it was an integral part of that worship. It is this that makes the prophetic metaphor of the land committing harlotry with Baal such an apt and forceful one.

11. *pilgrimages and new moons...sabbaths and festivals* are all words which are elsewhere applied to the celebrations of orthodox Israelite religion. What Hosea was faced with was not two distinct religions, co-existing in the same land, each with its own festivals and holy days, but a single religion

which had incorporated practices both from Israel's old national religion and the Baalism of the Canaanites.

When Hosea uses the metaphor of marriage he is not thinking of the modern European variety but of an ancient and eastern one. The husband's relation to his wife in Hosea's society was one not only of love but of authority. He had large powers of discipline over her, and the wife expressed her love for her husband primarily by obeying him. This explains how it is that Hosea not only interweaves the themes of love and judgement very closely in his work, but how he can use the analogy of marriage to convey both of them.   ✷

A SECOND HONEYMOON

But now listen,   14
I will woo her, I will go with her into the wilderness
     and comfort her:
     there I will restore her vineyards,   15
     turning the Vale of Trouble into the Gate of Hope,[a]
     and there she will answer as in her youth,
         when she came up out of Egypt.
On that day she[b] shall call me 'My husband'   16
     and shall no more call me 'My Baal';[c]
and I will wipe from her lips the very names of the 17
         Baalim;
     never again shall their names be heard.
     This is the very word of the LORD.[d]

✷ 14. *I will woo her*: the word translated 'woo' is a strong one, 'to appeal irresistibly', or even, in some contexts, 'to seduce'. God and Israel spent their honeymoon in the wilder-

[a] turning...Hope: *or* Emek-achor to Pethah-tikvah.
[b] *So Sept.; Heb.* you.   [c] *Also means* My husband.
[d] This...LORD: *transposed from after* On that day *in verse 16.*

ness. It is there that God will take her back and make a new beginning. *and comfort her:* the Hebrew is literally, 'and speak to her heart', a telling phrase.

15. *I will restore her vineyards:* Israel will again be allotted the fruitful land she was allotted before. The word 'vineyard' in Hebrew literature is a very evocative one. It is frequently a romantic or a sexual image. See, for example, the Song of the Vineyard, Isa. 5, and Song of Songs 7: 11–13.

Last time there was a setback. *the Vale of Trouble* (Achor) is the place where Achan was put to death for an act of disobedience and treachery which jeopardized the fulfilment of God's promises (Josh. 7). It is a valley leading up from Jericho into the heart of the land. But Israel's way into the land this time will not be fraught with trouble but sustained by hope. Hosea's fondness for playing on the significance of places comes out strongly here.

she will answer: 'answer' is a key word in Hosea, a fact which is not easy to bring out in translation, for it cannot always be rendered by the same English word. Perhaps 'respond' would be adequate in most contexts. Response is what Hosea, and Hosea's God, are always hoping for.

16–17. The word 'baal' in Hebrew had a number of associated meanings:

(1) It had a range of ordinary, secular meanings, e.g. 'master', 'owner', 'lord', 'husband'.

(2) It was a divine title. At one stage apparently any god could be thus described. The most prominent Canaanite god was properly 'baal Hadad', i.e. 'the lord Hadad', and in all likelihood Israel's God was known as 'baal Yahweh', 'the lord Yahweh'.

(3) But the title came to be restricted principally to heathen deities, so that one could speak of 'the baals', as Hosea does in 2: 13 and 2: 17. In this sense the phrase 'the baals' might properly be regarded as the equivalent of 'gods', with a small 'g'.

(4) There is an even more restricted use. In English the

word 'lord' is basically quite a general one, but if in a religious context we speak of 'the Lord' we mean the one and only God. Something similar happened to the word 'baal'. It came to be applied narrowly to the most prominent of the Canaanite gods, so that 'Baal' becomes virtually a proper name.

(5) Because of this, orthodox Israelites came to regard it as a dirty word, and Hosea is here asserting either, that it will no longer be allowed to cause confusion by being applied to Israel's national God, or, that it will cease to be used even in innocent contexts. ✳

THE NEW RELATIONSHIP

Then I will make a covenant on behalf of Israel with 18 the wild beasts, the birds of the air, and the things that creep on the earth, and I will break bow and sword and weapon of war and sweep them off the earth, so that all living creatures may lie down without fear. I will betroth 19 you to myself for ever, betroth you in lawful wedlock with unfailing devotion and love; I will betroth you to 20 myself to have and to hold, and you shall know the LORD. At that time I will give answer, says the LORD, I will 21 answer for the heavens and they will answer for the earth, and the earth will answer for the corn, the new wine, and 22 the oil, and they will answer for Jezreel. Israel shall be my 23 new sowing in the land, and I will show love to Lo-ruhamah and say to Lo-ammi, 'You are my people', and he will say, 'Thou art my God.'

✳ 18. The ideas in this verse are characteristic of the later post-exilic period. Some editor, looking forward to the end of the world and the establishment of the reign of peace, has added the verse, and added also, perhaps, the phrases 'on that day' and 'at that time' in verses 16 and 21. But the main content of verses 19–23 is typical of Hosea. The prophet is still talking of the new start which God will make with his bride.

19. *I will betroth you...*: betrothal is not merely the preliminary to marriage, it is the marriage itself. After it nothing remains but the consummation. A betrothed woman, even if consummation has not taken place, is regarded in Israelite law exactly like a married one. *I will betroth you to myself for ever*: it will not be the sort of casual union which Baal indulged in. *in lawful wedlock* is a paraphrase, but a good one. The Hebrew literally reads, 'in righteousness and in judgement', which in this context means, 'according to the proper forms of law and custom'; again a contrast with the irregular relationships countenanced in Baal-worship. *with unfailing devotion*: the phrase *unfailing devotion* represents a single Hebrew word, *ḥesed*. Hebrew has a number of different words for 'love'. This word *ḥesed* has no sexual overtones at all. It is not so much 'affection' as 'unshakable attachment'. The word which the N.E.B. does render in this passage by 'love' is again not a sexual word. It is often used of parental love, or of the kind of tenderness spontaneously called forth by what is small, or hurt, or cuddly. 'Tenderness' would perhaps be a good alternative translation.

20. *to have and to hold* is an allusive phrase, an echo of our own familiar marriage service, but not closely corresponding to the original, which has a word commonly translated 'in faithfulness'. *and you shall know the LORD*: the verb 'to know' in Hebrew is rich in overtones. It can in some contexts mean 'to have sexual intercourse with'. No gross meaning is intended here, but the prophet, following in his mind the ritual of the marriage, may be referring obliquely to the next stage; promises, betrothal, and now consummation.

22–3. And the result, naturally, is fertility, *the corn, the new wine, and the oil*. Note again the theme of response. When Israel responds to God, then the heavens will respond (with rain) and the earth will respond (by producing grain and fruit). ✳

88

A SECOND ACCOUNT OF HOSEA'S MARRIAGE

The LORD said to me,   3 1[a]

Go again and love a woman
loved by another man, an adulteress,
and love her as I, the LORD, love the Israelites
although they resort to other gods
and love the raisin-cakes offered to their idols.

So I got her back[b] for fifteen pieces of silver, a homer of 2
barley and a measure of wine;[c] and I said to her,   3

Many a long day you shall live in my house
and not play the wanton,
and have no intercourse with a man, nor I with you.

For the Israelites shall live many a long day   4
without king or prince,
without sacrifice or sacred pillar,
without image[d] or household gods;[e]
but after that they will again seek   5
the LORD their God and David their king,
and turn anxiously to the LORD for his bounty in days
to come.

* Chapter 3 tells us things about Hosea's marriage which the
account in chapter 1 had no reason to mention. It tells us, in
passing, what was the bride-price the prophet paid, but its
main interest is in the period of quarantine, or probation,
which the prophet inflicted on the bride. Hosea here uses his
marriage to make a prophecy about the collapse of the nation.

[a] *Chapter 3 is probably misplaced and should follow* 1: 9.
[b] got her back: *or* bought her.   [c] wine: *so Sept.; Heb.* barley.
[d] *Heb.* ephod.   [e] *Heb.* teraphim.

It will be deprived of its monarchy and governed no longer by its native rulers. It will be deprived of its religious observances and festivals. But this is not to be the end. Beyond the period of deprivation there is hope of a renewal; a renewal of the covenant relationship with God, a restoration of his favour.

1. On the N.E.B.'s note to this verse see p. 76. *Go again:* see p. 76. *and love a woman:* this word, yet another of the Hebrew words for 'love', does sometimes have a sexual connotation (in contrast with the other words dealt with above, p. 88) but it is also used very broadly; like our own English word 'love', in fact. *the raisin-cakes* were a delicacy, made of pressed grapes and flour, and eaten characteristically at the time of the Autumn Festival, which was the time of the grape harvest. They seem to have associations with Canaanite ritual. Figurines of the goddess Astarte have been found on some archaeological sites, showing the goddess holding a round, flat object which may well represent a raisin-cake (though some see it as a tambourine). The words *offered to their idols* are an explanatory addition by the N.E.B. translators. They correspond to nothing in the original.

2. *So I got her back:* N.E.B. note, 'bought her'. If this commentary is correct in concluding that chapters 1 and 3 describe the same event, the rendering in the note must be preferred. 'I bought her' would then refer to the payment of the bride-price to the girl's father. The translation *I got her back* assumes that Gomer, whom the prophet had married in chapter 1, had left her husband and fallen into slavery. The particular Hebrew word used does not help us to solve the problem. It is so odd in its form that it is not even certain which verb it is meant to be. It could be meant as a part of the verb 'to acknowledge': 'so I acknowledged her as mine'. If it does represent the verb 'to buy' it is a rather rare synonym; so rare that we cannot say for certain whether it could convey the meaning 'buy back', 'redeem', or whether it could only mean 'buy' (for the first time). By the same token, we cannot

be sure that it could be used in the sense 'offer the bride price', which the interpretation followed here would demand.

fifteen pieces of silver: i.e. fifteen shekels. Thirty shekels was the valuation of a female slave (Exod. 21: 32), but fifty shekels the compensation to a girl's father by a man who rapes her (Deut. 22: 29). By these standards the price paid by the prophet is fairly modest. Micah's priest (Judg. 17: 10) is paid ten shekels a year plus his clothes and keep. This suggests that if Hosea was a peasant farmer the price would nevertheless be felt as a considerable sum. *A homer of barley* was about four hundred litres or fifteen cubic feet. 'Homer', by derivation, means an ass-load. 'Measure', in the phrase *measure of wine*, is a unique word. It is traditionally taken to be half a homer, but we do not really know.

4. It is difficult for us to appreciate the enormous import-ance attached in the ancient world to the king. He was some-times felt to sustain not only the fabric of the state but of the world itself. On his health and vigour, and on his correct performance of his duties (especially his religious duties), de-pended not only the well-being of the nation but the regu-larity of the seasons and the fertility of the land. For a nation to be, therefore, *without king or prince*, and without any of the proper apparatus for sustaining its religious life, was for it to be defunct, or at least in chaos.

The *sacred pillar* was an upright stone, probably representing the male principle of deity. Every Canaanite shrine had one, or, more usually, several. It is possible that they were smeared with the fat and blood of the sacrifices (cp. Gen. 28: 18). *image* (footnote, *ephod*): some texts which mention the ephod make it clear that it was a garment. The infant Samuel wore one made of linen, and the ephod associated in later times with the high priest is generally assumed also to have been a garment. But other references to the ephod are inconsistent with this and suggest some sort of object used in divination. The word evidently had more than one meaning. *household gods* (footnote, *teraphim*): the Hebrew word undoubtedly refers to some kind of images. The teraphim which Rachel stole (Gen. 31: 19–35) were small enough to be hidden by being sat on. David's teraphim (1 Sam. 19: 9–17) seem to have been of roughly human size and shape, since they were tucked up in bed to make it look as if someone was asleep there. (Other interpretations of this passage are possible, however. See the commentary on 1 Samuel in this series.)

The surprising thing is that Hosea, who is very sensitive to religious irregularities, seems to imply that the *sacred pillar* and the *teraphim* are legitimate cult objects, and that for Israel to be deprived of them would be a calamity. In later times, of course, the sacred pillar was regarded as a heathen object, and images of every sort were rejected. Most of us have a fairly clear idea of what 'normal' Jewish religion regarded as acceptable belief or practice. For example, we know that it rejected all forms of idolatry and polytheism, and insisted that laws relating to circumcision, the sabbath, festivals and sacrifices were strictly kept. It is very easy to fall into the assumption that these standards were subscribed to in Israel from the beginning. But in fact no decisive step in laying down firm religious standards seems to have been taken until the end of the seventh century, when Josiah carried through his reform (2 Kings 22–3). And the Jewish norms with which we are familiar were not worked out with any thoroughness until the exile. In Hosea's day it would probably not have been possible to say what 'normal' Israelite religion was. A diversity of religious practice existed, and there were no standards of orthodoxy generally agreed.

5. *but after that they will again seek the LORD their God and David their king:* did Hosea really say this? We have seen reason to believe that Hosea regarded the separation of the two halves of the nation as a mistake, and that he looked forward to reunion (see notes on 1: 4 and 1: 11). It is not totally impossible that he should have expected this to involve the submission of the north to the house of David. During Hosea's lifetime the northern monarchy was in a chaotic state, with

dynasties changing rapidly and political assassination being
the order of the day. Throughout all this the dynasty of David
remained unperturbed. This situation could readily be interpreted as a vindication of the Davidic house against the un-
stable monarchy of Israel.

However, Hosea elsewhere seems to be against *all* kingship,
and to regard the institution of the monarchy as a mistake in
the beginning (see 8: 4, 9: 9, 10: 9–10, and especially 13: 10–
11). There are two possible interpretations of Hosea's attitude:

(1) He thinks it is a pity that the monarchy was ever instituted, but since it does exist, he is prepared to settle for reunion under Davidic rule. The idea that the monarchy was
a concession by God to Israel's weakness, but nevertheless
a divine instrument, is implied by other Old Testament writers.
Hos. 3: 4, which speaks of the deprivation of its kings as a
disaster for the land, favours this interpretation of Hosea's
mind.

(2) Hosea really is opposed to all monarchy. He visualizes
any reunion as taking place under a different system of government (see note on 1: 5). The words *and David their king* in this
verse have therefore been added by a Judaean editor. *

God's case against Israel

A new section of the book begins here. It starts with a collection of oracles bearing on God's accusation of Israel. The first
batch, which continues into chapter 5, is concerned largely
with the priesthood. There is no general agreement about
where one oracle ends and another begins, and the N.E.B.'s
paragraphing represents only one possible point of view.

INDICTMENT OF PRIESTS AND PEOPLE

4   Hear the word of the LORD, O Israel;
   for the LORD has a charge to bring against the people of
      the land:
      There is no good faith or mutual trust,
      no knowledge of God in the land,
2   oaths are imposed and broken, they kill and rob;
      there is nothing but adultery and licence;[a]
      one deed of blood after another.
3   Therefore the land shall be dried up,
      and all who live in it shall pine away,
      and with them the wild beasts and the birds of the air;
      even the fish shall be swept from the sea.
4   But it is not for any man to bring a charge,
      it is not for him to prove a case;
      the quarrel with you, false priest, is mine.

5   Priest?[b] By day and by night you blunder on,
      you and the prophet with you.
6   My people are ruined for lack of knowledge;
      your own countrymen are brought to ruin.[c]
     You have rejected knowledge,
      and I will reject you from serving me as priest.
     You have forgotten the teaching of God,
      and I, your God, will forget your sons.

[a] and licence: *prob. rdg.; Heb.* they exceed.
[b] the quarrel...Priest?: *prob. rdg.; Heb.* and your people are like those who quarrel with a priest.
[c] My people...ruin: *or* Your mother (Israel) is destroyed, my people destroyed for lack of knowledge.

✻ The text of these verses is in serious disorder, a number of lines making very dubious sense indeed. Verses 1-4 are an introduction, announcing the accusation against the whole nation, but verses 5-6 make it clear that the priests are the chief offenders.

1. *Hear the word of the LORD* is a common introductory formula for a prophetic oracle, though not common in Hosea. The phrase is of the kind used by court heralds when making an announcement having the king's authority. For the body of the oracle the prophet drops into a different style, that of the law court. He is making a public announcement that a case is to be heard, *for the LORD has a charge to bring against the people of the land.* The charges sound like general ones of moral laxity, but they are more specific than they seem. God was believed to have made a covenant with his people, first at Sinai and then at Shechem, and this covenant involved certain conditions, one summary of which is in the ten commandments. Hosea's words are carefully chosen allusions to those famous conditions. The action which God is bringing is a specific one of breach of contract.

Good faith and *mutual trust* are exactly the virtues demanded by the covenant. The terms are two-edged. They refer not only to good faith and mutual trust between one Israelite and another, in their commercial and civic life, but to good faith between all Israelites and God. The *mutual trust* is that same 'unfailing devotion' (*ḥesed*) which was mentioned in 2: 19. *Knowledge of God* is a very comprehensive and rich phrase. It involves piety, the proper fulfilment of religious duties. It involves uprightness of moral life, probity, both on an individual and social level. And it involves spirituality, i.e. an inward conviction of the reality of God. Knowledge of God is something that can be taught. It is taught by giving instruction about the terms of the covenant; by reciting or explaining the law in which they are embodied; and by recounting the saving acts of God on which the covenant rests. All this teaching it was the priests' job to give. If, then, the covenant is ignored and the covenantal virtues not practised, the primary responsibility must lie with the priesthood who have failed to impart the 'teaching of God' (verse 6).

Note that Hosea does not suggest that priestly religion is irrelevant or that priests ought to be abolished. He assumes their work to be vital, and his complaint is simply that they do it badly. That work is primarily one of teaching the religious traditions. In the pre-exilic period the offering of sacrifices was not the most prominent part of priestly duties.

2. *oaths are imposed and broken, they kill and rob; there is nothing but adultery and licence, one deed of blood after another*: these are clear allusions to the ten commandments, which Hosea evidently knew in something like their present form.

3. *Therefore the land shall be dried up, and all who live in it shall pine away*: the Baal-worshippers believed that if their fertility ceremonies were not carried out according to custom the land would wither and nature decay. Hosea asserts that any withering or decay would rather be the result of breaking the covenant with God. Immorality is what rots the fabric of the universe.

4. This verse is very obscure, and translating it is little more than guesswork. It does seem to make a transition between the accusation of the nation in verses 1–3 and that of the priesthood in 5–6.

5. The N.E.B. has altered the word order here, but some such expedient is necessary in order to get sense out of the verse. To translate the verb as a present, *you blunder*, makes the verse part of the indictment. It could as readily be translated as future and rendered, 'you shall stumble', which would make it part not of the indictment but of the sentence. *you and the prophet with you*: the linking of priest and prophet is interesting. There were several different sorts of prophets with different functions and outlooks. The reference here would be to the kind of prophet who was on the paid staff of a sanctuary.

6. Amos prophesied disaster for one priestly individual and

his family (Amos 7: 17), but Hosea announces God's rejection of an entire priesthood. The words used are similar to the
rejection formula applied to the house of Saul (1 Sam. 15: 23),
and in content are reminiscent of the rejection of the priesthood of Eli (1 Sam. 2: 27-36). These words are bound to
affect our assessment of Hosea's attitude to the whole question
of the independence of the Northern Kingdom. His rejection
of the northern priesthood seems to be all of a piece with his
questioning of the legitimacy of the monarchy and his asser-
tions that it does not enjoy divine favour.

Up to verse 6 the priesthood has been addressed in the
second person singular, as though the prophet were speaking
to the head of the priestly caste. At verse 7 he changes to the
third person, suggesting that we have moved into a different
oracle altogether. ✻

MORE ABOUT THE PRIESTHOOD

The more priests there are, the more they sin against 7
    me;
their dignity I will turn into dishonour.
    They feed on the sin of my people   8
and batten on their iniquity.
But people and priest shall be treated alike.   9
I will punish them for their conduct
and repay them for their deeds:
    they shall eat but never be satisfied,   10
behave wantonly but their lust will never be
    overtaxed,
    for they have forsaken the LORD
    to give themselves to sacred prostitution.   11

✻ At several places in this passage the Hebrew original is very
corrupt. Sometimes we can make an intelligent guess at what

was originally written, but there are one or two points at which we must admit that the writer's intentions are now irrecoverable.

7. *their dignity I will turn into dishonour*: some ancient translators apparently read 'their dignity *they* have turned...'.

8. *They feed on the sin of my people and batten on their iniquity*: it is difficult to say precisely what the prophet means by this. It may be suggesting that the priests connive at abuses which they should have been the first to prevent, and perhaps make profit out of them too.

9. *But people and priest shall be treated alike*: the Hebrew says simply, and cryptically, 'But it shall be, like people, like priest.' This means either (1) that God will inflict the same judgement on them (which is what the N.E.B. implies), or possibly (2) that the people are becoming as corrupt as their priesthood, being faced with such bad examples, or (3) the reverse, that the priests behave no better than common men.

10. *they...behave wantonly but their lust will never be overtaxed*: the N.E.B. makes this a statement parallel to the one in the previous line. Just as their greed is never satisfied, neither is their lust. But the verb translated *overtaxed* is ambiguous. A more traditional rendering is on the lines, 'They play the harlot but shall not increase.' This would make sense in the context, since the object of sexual acts in ritual was to secure fertility. If God cannot stop them indulging in these reprehensible practices he can at least ensure that they do not produce the desired result. ✳

ISRAEL'S SORDID WORSHIP

12 New wine and old steal my people's wits:[a]
 they ask advice from a block of wood
 and take their orders from a fetish;[b]
 for a spirit of wantonness has led them astray

[a] steal...wits: *or* embolden my people.   [b] *Lit.* stick.

and in their lusts they are unfaithful to their God.
Your men sacrifice on mountain-tops   13
   and burn offerings on the hills,
   under oak and poplar
and the terebinth's pleasant shade.
Therefore your daughters play the wanton
   and your sons' brides commit adultery.
I will not punish your daughters for playing the   14
     wanton
   nor your sons' brides for their adultery,
because your men resort to wanton women
   and sacrifice with temple-prostitutes.
A people without understanding comes to grief;
   they are a mother turned wanton.   15
Bring no guilt-offering,*ᵃ* Israel;
do not come to Gilgal, Judah,
do not go up to Beth-aven to swear by the life of the
   Lᴏʀᴅ,
since Israel has run wild, wild as a heifer;   16
   and will the Lᴏʀᴅ now feed this people
   like lambs in a broad meadow?
Ephraim, keeping company with idols,   17
   has held a drunken orgy,*ᵇ*   18
     they have practised sacred prostitution,
   they have preferred dishonour to glory.*ᶜ*
The wind shall sweep them away, wrapped in its   19
     wings,
   and they will find their sacrifices a delusion.

[a] Bring no guilt-offering: *prob. rdg.; Heb.* Let him not be guilty.
[b] a drunken orgy: *prob. rdg.; Heb. unintelligible.*
[c] to glory: *prob. rdg., cp. Sept.; Heb.* her shields.

✻ Hosea turns momentarily from the priesthood, but his mind is still on the cult.

12. *New wine and old steal my people's wits:* it was at the Autumn Festival, the vintage feast, that the wildest junketings went on. *they ask advice from a block of wood and take their orders from a fetish:* there may be some reference here to special methods of divining by throwing sticks into the air, but more likely the words *block of wood* and *fetish* (literally 'stick') simply derogatory terms for idols in general or for the asherah in particular. The asherah was a cult object taking the form of a wooden pole, a companion to the sacred pillar (see note on 3: 4) and a symbol of the female principle of deity.

In the phrase *a spirit of wantonness has led them astray* the word 'spirit' means primarily 'an overpowering urge'. 'Spirit' to our minds suggests something immaterial and non-physical. To the Hebrew speaker it meant primarily something strong. The spirit, whether a good one or a bad one, comes from outside a man and overpowers him, irresistibly. The *spirit of wantonness* is thus a kind of madness. The prophet cannot explain the people's irrational behaviour in any other way.

13. *Mountain-tops* were the traditional places for Canaanite worship. When shrines were built in the lowlands they were still called 'high places' and were often constructed on an artificial mound. Canaanite shrines generally had few buildings. They did frequently have a tree or a grove of trees. This explains the reference to *oak and poplar and the terebinth's pleasant shade*. Palestinian weather is much more predictable than the weather in most of Europe and worship was therefore primarily an outdoor affair. *your daughters play the wanton and your sons' brides commit adultery:* it has been suggested that this refers to an initiation rite in which girls were obliged to prostitute themselves at the sanctuary before marriage. Such rites certainly were customary among some peoples of the ancient world but we have no direct evidence that they were observed in Palestine.

14. The women, says Hosea, cannot be criticized, because

their menfolk do just the same. What is sauce for the gander is sauce for the goose. The word translated *temple-prostitutes* means basically 'holy women'. This casts an interesting light on what the word 'holy' originally meant. It had nothing to do with morals. 'Holy' meant 'set aside for sacred use'. The temple-prostitute was called a holy woman because she was used in religious acts, exactly as the tongs on the altar were holy tongs. One of the peculiarities of the Old Testament prophets was that they insisted that nothing could deserve the title 'holy' unless it was morally as well as ritually worthy. The fact that we all now take this for granted is a measure of their success. *A people without understanding comes to grief* was probably a current proverb, though whether Hosea himself quoted it or whether some pious scribe wrote it in the margin we cannot be sure.

15. A very obscure verse. The traditional rendering is, 'Though you play the harlot, Israel, let not Judah become guilty.' This makes it look suspiciously like a warning inserted by a Judaean editor. Hosea does elsewhere address Judah, but not in terms like these. The N.E.B. has transferred the opening phrase of verse 15, 'though (you) play the harlot', to the end of verse 14. The uneven length of the poetic lines suggests this expedient and the transfer makes for a tidier-looking poetic structure. But the transferred phrase has to be emended to make it fit into its new context in verse 14. The N.E.B. has read 'though' as 'mother' (a very easy change in Hebrew; *'em* instead of *'im*) but produced a somewhat abrupt piece of Hebrew: *they are a mother turned wanton*. A more popular emendation makes the whole last line of verse 14 read, 'A people without understanding comes to grief with a harlot.'

Gilgal: the note on Gilgal in Amos 4: 4 also applies here. *Beth-aven*, 'house of trouble' or 'house of wickedness', is a nasty nickname for Bethel ('house of God'), the country's principal sanctuary.

16. *Israel has run wild, wild as a heifer; and will the LORD now feed this people like lambs in a broad meadow?* the text does,

up to a point, make sense, but it contains a rather improbable confusion of metaphors and whether it represents what was originally written is doubtful.

17–18. Any translation of these verses has to be based on a more or less hypothetical reconstruction of the text. If it really does refer to a *drunken orgy* this is not surprising. Isaiah, speaking at about the same time, refers to the leaders of northern Israel as 'the drunkards of Ephraim' and gives us a brief but repulsive description of an orgy in Isa. 28: 7–8. Hosea very frequently designates the Northern Kingdom as *Ephraim* rather than 'Israel'. Ephraim and Manasseh were the two sons of Joseph, and the tribes (more properly half-tribes) of Ephraim and Manasseh were by far the most important ones in the north. Cp. the note on Amos 5: 6. But by the eighth century the Manassites had declined, much of their land being east of Jordan where it was very exposed to Syrian attacks. It was therefore natural at this period to regard 'Ephraim' as standing for the whole of the Northern Kingdom. ✶

INDICTMENT OF PRIESTS AND KINGS

5   Hear this, you priests,
    and listen, all Israel; let the royal house mark my words.
      Sentence is passed on you;
    for you have been a snare at Mizpah,
    and a net spread out on Tabor.
2   The rebels! they have shown base ingratitude,
    but I will punish them all.
3   I have cared for Ephraim
    and I have not neglected Israel;
    but now Ephraim has played the wanton
    and Israel has defiled himself.
4   Their misdeeds have barred their way back to their
    God;

for a wanton spirit is in them,
    and they care nothing for the LORD.
Israel's arrogance cries out against him;   5
*a*Ephraim's guilt is his undoing,
    and Judah no less is undone.
They go with sacrifices of sheep and cattle   6
to seek the LORD, but do not find him.
    He has withdrawn himself from them;
    for they have been unfaithful to him,   7
and their sons are bastards.
Now an invader shall devour their fields.

* 1. The address to priests and people continues, but now
with the addition of the *royal house*. Possibly verses 1–2 are
a self-contained oracle and verse 3 makes a fresh beginning.

2. *The rebels! they have shown base ingratitude:* the Hebrew
is meaningless, and guesses as to what it originally said vary
widely. As it stands it contains the word 'slaughter' and a
word which could mean 'rebels' or 'revolt'. If, in the disturbed years following the death of Jeroboam II, the prophet
had something to say about rebels and slaughter it would be
natural enough. Another popular reconstruction produces a
line closely parallel in thought to the preceding two: 'They
are a pit made deep at Shittim.' Thus the prophet would be
likening Israel to three different types of snare: a bird trap
(at Mizpah), a net (at Tabor) and a pit, for larger game (at
Shittim). The three places may have been chosen as ones associated with Baal worship, though in the case of Mizpah and
Tabor there is not much evidence for this. Shittim is near
Baal-peor where Israel fell into idolatry on the way to the
promised land (Num. 25).

Verses 3–7 are concerned with abuses in worship.

4. *Their misdeeds have barred their way back to their God:* what

[a] Prob. rdg.; Heb. *prefixes* Israel.

Hosea means by this is made clear in his next statement about the *wanton spirit* (see note on 4: 12). They are so habituated to wrongdoing that they could not stop if they wanted to. They are possessed, and no longer under their own control. Compare the similar statement in Isa. 59: 2. *they care nothing for the LORD* is literally 'they do not know the LORD'. They no longer have any real consciousness of him (see note on 4: 1). And this is in spite of the fact that the Lord has always *cared for Ephraim* ('known Ephraim') and *not neglected Israel* (verse 3).

5. *Israel's arrogance cries out against him:* literally 'answers against him', a technical legal idiom meaning 'accuses him'. *and Judah no less is undone:* the mention of Judah may or may not have been originally included by the prophet, but as it stands the verse provides a good introduction to verses 8–15, which do deal with both halves of the nation.

6. *He has withdrawn himself from them* echoes a theme found in the Baal myths and elsewhere in ancient near eastern religion, the theme of the withdrawal or the death of God. The god dies or disappears and has to be sought and brought back by the carrying out of the correct ritual. But, says Hosea, no amount of ritual or sacrifice will bring back Israel's God. He has withdrawn because of his people's unfaithfulness and can be brought back only by their repentance (cp. verse 15).

When the God of Israel withdraws from his people and is no longer accessible to their prayers the situation is serious indeed (cp. Isa. 1: 15, Jer. 11: 14). God in the Old Testament is normally characterized by his accessibility. It is usually assumed that he can be appealed to at all times and in all places and by all men. Isa. 65: 24 is a typical statement of his readiness, even eagerness, to respond to men. 'Before they call to me, I will answer, and while they are still speaking I will listen.'

7. *Now an invader shall devour their fields:* the original reads, improbably, 'Now the new moon shall devour...' Some defend this and try to find a ritual significance in it, or interpret, 'within a month' the end will come. ✶

THE SYRO-EPHRAIMITE WAR

What follows is probably a collection of sayings uttered at various times during the Syro-Ephraimite war. The sayings on this theme perhaps end at 5: 14, though some critics prolong the collection as far as 6: 6.

In 734 B.C. Israel and Syria, who were old enemies, decided to make common cause against the Assyrians. They tried to force Judah to join them, and when Judah, under king Ahaz, resisted the suggestion they attacked Judah and besieged Jerusalem. Judah, in desperation, appealed to the Assyrians, who were only too ready to intervene. In the end Syria, Israel and Judah were all losers. The events are described in 2 Kings 16: 5–9 and in Isa. 7.

Hosea and Isaiah both have something to say about the affair. Though their countries were on different sides and pursuing opposite policies they have broadly the same thing to say. Playing power-politics is no cure for the nation's ills. In the long run she can only suffer as a result. If the nation were to get its relationship with God right the politics would take care of themselves. Judah tries to buy Assyria off, Israel tries to fight her. Both are wasting their time, say the prophets. Assyria is not the real enemy. She is only a weapon in the hand of God, and he is the one whom the nation must satisfy.

> Blow the trumpet in Gibeah,   8
>   the horn in Ramah,
>   raise the battle-cry in Beth-aven:
>   'Benjamin, we are with you!'
> On the tribes of Israel I have proclaimed this unalterable 9
>   doom:
> on the day of punishment Ephraim shall be laid waste.
> The rulers of Judah act like men who move their neigh- 10
>   bour's boundary;

on them will I pour out my wrath like a flood.

11   Ephraim is an oppressor trampling on justice,
      doggedly pursuing what is worthless.

12   But I am a festering sore to Ephraim,
        a canker to the house of Judah.

13   So when Ephraim found that he was sick,
        Judah that he was covered with sores,
      Ephraim went to Assyria,
      he went in haste to the Great King;
      but he has no power to cure you
      or to heal your sores.

14   Yes indeed, I will be fierce as a panther to Ephraim,
        fierce as a lion to Judah –
      I will maul the prey and go,
      carry it off beyond hope of rescue – I, the LORD.

✻ 8. *Gibeah*...*Ramah*...*Beth-aven* (Bethel) are all near the southern border of Israel, in Benjaminite territory, and therefore most exposed to attack from Judah. Although initially it was Israel who did the attacking Judah doubtless counter-attacked when Assyria entered the war on her side. On *Beth-aven* see note on 4: 15.

10. *The rulers of Judah act like men who move their neighbour's boundary:* apparently Judah took the opportunity to expropriate territory. There was an area of land between the two countries whose possession was disputed throughout the period of the divided kingdom.

In Palestine fields and farms were marked off from each other not by substantial fences but simply by boundary stones. To move a boundary stone by a few feet was difficult to detect and an easy way of gaining land. In all societies crimes which are easy to get away with attract special opprobrium, for society's only defence against such misdeeds is a strong contempt for those who commit them. See, for example, the curse in Deut. 27: 17.

11. The Hebrew of this verse is again difficult. Instead of *doggedly pursuing what is worthless*, some suggest that we read, 'insisting on going along with his enemy'. This would turn the verse into a criticism of Israel for making common cause with her traditional enemy, Syria, against her sister nation.

13. *Ephraim went to Assyria...*: it is doubtful what the prophet is referring to here. The words would very aptly describe the action of Judah when she appealed for Assyrian help against Israel and Syria, but it is difficult to think of an occasion when the northerners made such an appeal. Some have suggested that it refers to Menahem's bribing of Tiglath Pileser, mentioned in 2 Kings 15: 19, or to Israel's capitulation after the Assyrian overthrow of her Syrian allies. But neither of these episodes could readily be described as 'going for healing'. *he has no power to cure you*: the notion of a king as a possible healer would not sound odd to ancient ears. Kings were repositories of power, and power to govern, power to distinguish truth from falsehood, power to heal, were regarded as only different manifestations of the same thing. Naaman, sent to Israel for healing, goes automatically in the first instance to the king (2 Kings 5).

14. *I will be fierce as a panther*: the comparison of God with a wild animal is not the sort that would occur to the modern religious mind. But animal gods, or statues and pictures of gods with animal features, were commonplace in the ancient near east. By these means ancient man conveyed something of his feeling of the dread and power of deity. The Old Testament does not scorn such imagery, but it confines it to literature and forbids it in the plastic arts (see also 13: 4–8). ✳

✓

A PSALM OF PENITENCE

15   I will go away and return to my place
        until in their horror they seek me,
            and look earnestly for me in their distress.

6   Come, let us return to the LORD;
        for he has torn us and will heal us,
            he has struck us and he will bind up our wounds;
2   after two days he will revive us,
        on the third day he will restore us,
            that in his presence we may live.
3   Let us humble ourselves, let us strive to know the LORD,
        whose justice dawns like*a* morning light,*b*
        and its dawning is as sure as the sunrise.
        It will come to us like a shower,
            like spring rains that water the earth.

MHⱭ
245.

* Many, both ancient translators and modern scholars, thus attach 5:15 to the beginning of chapter 6. 5:15 does not follow naturally on 5: 14 but makes a good introduction to the little psalm in 6: 1–3.

15. What is *my place*? It is probably the Lord's original home in the Sinai desert. He accompanied Israel from there when they entered Canaan, but in some circles it was felt for a long time that this was still his real home, and that when the nation was threatened he had to march up from Sinai to their help.

In near eastern mythology the withdrawal of God is not a voluntary one (cp. the comments on 5: 6). It is a defeat by the forces of death and infertility. But for Hosea the withdrawal of God is deliberate. He withdraws his presence because his people are not worthy of it, and he waits for their

[a] whose...like: *prob. rdg.*, *cp. Sept.*; *Heb.* thy justice dawns.
[b] *Line transposed from end of verse 5.*

repentance. The words *until in their horror they seek me* follow
the reading of the Septuagint. The Hebrew reads, 'until they
acknowledge their guilt and seek me'.

1–3. This song of penitence is of a type used in worship,
especially in times of calamity. Many commentators regard the
song as an inadequate or shallow expression of penitence, on
which the prophet comments unfavourably in verses 4–6. But
a song which includes a summons to *strive to know the LORD*
(on knowledge of God see the note on 4: 1) can hardly be
described as shallow. If we separate 5: 15–6: 3 from what
follows there is no reason why it should not stand on its own
feet as a penitential psalm, expressing the very sentiments
which the prophet is trying to encourage. It is evidently
Hosea's own composition, for it contains some of his characteristic vocabulary. But he not only sticks closely to a traditional model, he introduces, equally characteristically, allusions to the familiar imagery of the Baal cult. The psalm has
been inserted at this point through an accident of vocabulary.
'I will maul the prey and go', in 5: 14, reminded the editor
of the words of this song, *For he has torn* (the words translated
'maul' and 'torn' are the same word in the Hebrew).

2. *on the third day he will restore us:* more than one nature
deity was believed to die and to rise again on the third day.
Hosea has put his own twist into the imagery. For him it is not
the God, but his worshippers, who need new life.

3. The God of Israel took over many of the characteristics
of the sun god, and language appropriate to the sun god is often
used in the Old Testament to describe him and his ways. But
for Hosea, as for the other Old Testament writers, the real
splendour of the rising God is seen in his justice. If he is a sun,
it is a 'sun of righteousness', *whose justice dawns like morning
light, and its dawning is as sure as the sunrise.* The *spring rains*
are the light rains which occur in March and April, just before
the harvest ripens. They are most important, since they give
the grain a chance to fill out before the long dry summer
begins. The other important rains are the light ones which

come in autumn, before the heavy winter rains proper, and which soften the ground to make ploughing possible. A good deal of Palestinian religious ritual was devoted to the task of ensuring that these rains were sufficient, but not too much. And in Canaanite religion the control of the rains was Baal's special prerogative and expertise. *

THE DEMAND FOR LOYALTY

4   O Ephraim, how shall I deal with you?
    How shall I deal with you, Judah?
    Your loyalty to me is like the morning mist,
    like dew that vanishes early.
5   Therefore have I lashed you through the prophets
        and torn you[a] to shreds with my words;
6   loyalty is my desire, not sacrifice,
        not whole-offerings but the knowledge of God.

* This oracle is not intimately connected with the preceding psalm, but was probably inserted here by the editor because, like the psalm, it ends with an appeal to pursue knowledge of God.

Hosea introduces one of his favourite images, that of the parent faced with the 'impossible' child. He conveys the parent's feeling of utter helplessness before a child who simply does not respond to his affection and concern.

5. *Therefore have I lashed you through the prophets and torn you to shreds with my words*: this translation represents, if anything, a softening of Hosea's language. Literally, what he says is, 'I have hewn you to pieces...and killed you...' Hosea is probably not thinking only of the verbal castigations which the prophets had inflicted on the people. He is thinking of physical punishments, such as plague, famine and war, which had come upon them following prophetic pronouncements.

[a] *Prob. rdg.; Heb.* them.

On the power of the prophetic word to accomplish its ends, see the note on Amos 7: 10.

6. It is not that Israel has failed to respond altogether. But her response is expressed in sacrifices and offerings, and this is not what God wants. Verse 6 is a famous denunciation of sacrifice. Cp. 8: 13. *loyalty is my desire, not sacrifice:* the precise force of the Hebrew idiom is disputed. It may plausibly be taken to mean, 'I want loyalty: I do not want sacrifice.' This would make it a total rejection of sacrificial worship. But some argue that it is intended simply as a statement of priorities, and that the appropriate translation is, 'Loyalty is my desire, *rather than* sacrifice.' Thus translated the words would not imply that God does not require sacrifice, but only that loyalty is much more important to him. Hosea's statement is strongly reminiscent of 1 Sam. 15: 22, 'Obedience is better than sacrifice, and to listen to him (God) than the fat of rams.' ✶

THE GEOGRAPHY OF SIN

At Admah*a* they have broken my covenant,	7
there they have played me false.	
Gilead is a haunt of evildoers,	8
marked by a trail of blood;	
like robbers lying in wait for a man,	9
priests are banded together	
to do murder on the road to Shechem;	
their deeds are outrageous.	
At Israel's sanctuary I have seen a horrible thing:	10
there Ephraim played the wanton	
and Israel defiled himself.	
And for you, too, Judah, comes a harvest of	11 *a*
reckoning.	

[a] At Admah: *prob. rdg.; Heb.* Like Adam.

✱ Here we have a kind of conducted tour of the places of Israel's disloyalty. Unfortunately some of the references seem to be to contemporary events of which we have no independent knowledge.

7. *Admah* is referred to by Hosea himself in 11: 8 as a place recently destroyed.

8. *Gilead*, we know, suffered badly at Assyrian hands when they attacked in 734 B.C., and was at that point taken out of Israelite control. Possibly, then, Hosea has picked out two places which had suffered recent calamity as places especially deserving of judgement.

9. The prophet now turns to two well-known sanctuary towns. *Shechem* was an ancient sanctuary, particularly important during the period before the monarchy. It is not clear whether Hosea is literally accusing the priests of complicity in the attempts of bandits to waylay pilgrims, or whether he is only using a simile, suggesting that what the priests are doing is no better than robbery. Malachi (3: 8) uses similar language, but makes it clear that the 'robbery' is the offering to God of less than his due.

10. *Israel's sanctuary* is almost certainly Bethel. The accusation against it is the one with which Hosea has already made us familiar, that sacred prostitution goes on there.

11. The final comment, *And for you, too, Judah, comes a harvest of reckoning*, is often suspected of being a later addition to the text. We cannot be certain that it is so. Hosea displays an interest in both halves of the nation, and is critical of both. ✱

Chapter 7 is held together by its general theme of the degeneracy of Israelite society. It probably consists of separate utterances of the prophet, delivered on different occasions, but there is little unanimity of opinion about where one ends and another begins.

THE BREAKDOWN OF LAW AND ORDER

When I would reverse the fortunes of my people,   11*b*
    when I would heal Israel,   7
    then the guilt of Ephraim stands revealed,
    and all the wickedness of Samaria;
    they have not kept faith.
They are thieves, they break into houses;[a]
they are robbers, they strip people in the street,
little thinking that I have their wickedness ever in mind.   2
    Now their misdeeds beset them
    and stare me in the face.

* 11*b*. *Reverse the fortunes* is a common Hebrew phrase. It often refers to the decisive act of salvation which was always looked forward to in the Autumn Festival. This 'day of the Lord' is what the people eagerly desire and the expectation of it is central to their worship. But their own behaviour forestalls its coming. In later times the coming act of salvation was identified with the restoration of the people from exile, and the phrase *reverse the fortunes* came to be applied narrowly to this expectation of return.

The open breakdown of law and order which these verses seem to picture fits in with what we know of the political situation in the twenty-five years or so between the death of Jeroboam II and the fall of Samaria to the Assyrians. There was a rapid succession of rulers and the situation became progressively more anarchic. *

[a] houses: *prob. rdg.; Heb. om.*

OF KINGS AND BAKERS

3   They win over the king with their wickedness
        and princes with their treachery,

4 lecherous all of them, hot as an oven over the fire
        which the baker does not stir
        after kneading the dough until it is proved.

5   On their[a] king's festal day the officers
        begin to be inflamed with wine,
        and he joins in the orgies of arrogant men;

6   for their hearts are heated by it[b] like an oven.
        While they are relaxed all night long
        their passion slumbers,
     but in the morning it flares up
        like a blazing fire;

7   they all grow feverish, hot as an oven,
        and devour their rulers.
     King after king falls from power,
     but not one of them calls upon me.

✳ **3.** *They win over the king with their wickedness*: literally, 'they make the king rejoice in their wickedness'. Another suggestion, involving a small alteration of the text, is 'they anoint kings in their wickedness'. This would make the words an assertion that the kings who came to the throne through assassination or *coup d'état* were not validly appointed and no good could come of them. The difficulty with this suggestion is that the verb 'anoint' would also have to govern the noun 'princes' in the next clause, and so far as we know 'princes' were not anointed.

    Verses 4–6 are in some respects obscure. This much we can

[a] *So Targ.; Heb.* our.
[b] are heated by it: *prob. rdg.; Heb.* draw near.

say for certain, however: the subject of the passage is the social situation and the political disturbances lying behind it. And the passage is held together by the metaphor of the oven. The principal point of the imagery seems to be a comparison between the intrigues of the politicians and a smouldering fire. When left alone the fire may look black and dead, but fierce heat is below the surface. It can be stirred into life at a moment's notice.

The type of oven which Hosea has in mind was a bell-shaped structure of clay, between half a metre and a metre in diameter. The fire, usually of dried grass (cp. Matt. 6: 30), was lit inside it, and when the oven was thoroughly heated the fire and ashes were swept out and the cakes plastered on to its walls and floor to bake as the oven cooled. There was also a smaller, portable type of domestic oven, made of pot, which stood among the ashes in the hearth.

The old suggestion that Hosea himself was a baker has no evidence to support it.

5. The Hebrew of this verse is virtually nonsense and the translation guesswork. The *king's festal day* is either the day of his coronation, or the New Year Festival at which, perhaps, he renewed his coronation vows. Some suggest that the meaning of the verse is that the politicians are intriguing against the king almost before they have got him on the throne.

7. *King after king falls from power.* They *devour their rulers.* A precise description of what was going on: four kings were assassinated in little more than a decade. ✱

THE HALF-BAKED NATION

Ephraim and his aliens make a sorry mixture;   8
Ephraim has become a cake half-baked.
    Foreigners fed on his strength,   9
      but he was unaware;

    even his grey hairs turned white,
      but he was unaware.

10   So Israel's arrogance cries out against them;
      but they do not return to the LORD their God
      nor seek him, in spite of it all.

11   Ephraim is a silly senseless pigeon,
      now calling upon Egypt, now turning to Assyria for
        help.

12   Wherever they turn, I will cast my net over them
      and will bring them down like birds on the wing;
      I will take them captive as soon as I hear them
        flocking.

✶ 8. *Ephraim and his aliens make a sorry mixture*: this presumably refers to religious apostasy, Israel having adopted unbecoming foreign ways. The *mixture* referred to is an oil and flour mix, used for making a kind of flat cake. This type of cake had to be turned when it was cooked on one side, otherwise it would be half burnt, half raw. Such a *cake half-baked* must have been an unpleasant object.

9. The repeated *but he was unaware* is literally, 'but he did not know'. Hosea's obsession with the idea of 'knowing' has already been noted (see comments on 2: 20 and 4: 1). The picture here is the pathetic one of a man declining into senility without realizing it or admitting the fact to himself. It is not easy, perhaps, for an individual to be unaware that he is in decline (though it does happen), but for a nation it is all too possible.

Hosea's exploitation of metaphor is masterly, though the Hebrew technique of using the same metaphor, in the same context, to make different and sometimes unrelated points is unfamiliar to us, and to our minds often confuses more than it clarifies. But like most literary conventions it makes sense once one realizes what the writer is doing.

11. A fresh image, that of the pigeon, is introduced. Palestine in the ancient world always lay between two great powers, the Egyptian and the Mesopotamian (the power in Mesopotamia was sometimes Assyria, sometimes Babylon, and, at later date, Persia). And her rulers were always tempted to play one off against the other, *now calling upon Egypt, now turning to Assyria for help*. This is always a dangerous game for small nations to play, though profitable if played well. Israel, on the whole, did not play it well, certainly not during Hosea's lifetime.

12. The obscure last line masks, one suspects, technical phrases used by fowlers, possibly referring to the use of decoys. At any rate, three ways of capturing birds seem to be referred to, netting, shooting (with bow or sling) and a third way about whose details we cannot be clear. The picture is of the pigeon, flapping ignorantly about, not knowing the lurking danger. So Israel, in her foreign diplomacy, flaps around, not knowing that God is waiting with the shotgun. *

A PERVERTED PEOPLE

Woe betide them, for they have strayed from me !   13
May disaster befall them for rebelling against me !
    I long to deliver them,
but they tell lies about me.
    There is no sincerity in their cry to me;   14
    for all their howling on their pallets
    and gashing of themselves[a] over corn and new wine,
      they are turning away from me.
Though I support them, though I give them strength 15
      of arm,
    they plot evil against me.
      Like a bow gone slack,   16

[a] gashing of themselves: *so many MSS.; others* rolling about.

they relapse into the worship of their high god;[a]
their talk is all lies,[b]
and so their princes shall fall by the sword.

✻ 13. Israel has still not learnt the true nature of his own God. *They tell lies* about him. The tense of the verb *I long to deliver them* is ambiguous. It could mean 'I have delivered them again and again'.

14. They insist on treating him like one of the fertility gods, *howling on their pallets and gashing...themselves over corn and new wine*. This is a reference to the ritual lamentation over the dead Baal. The self-mutilation is well attested in the story of Elijah on Carmel (1 Kings 18: 28).

16. *Like a bow gone slack:* the compound bow in common use in the ancient near east was a formidable and sophisticated weapon of laminated construction. But the more complex the instrument the more readily it can go wrong, and references to archers whose weapons failed them in the crisis of battle are not rare in ancient literature. Cp. the complaint of Teucer in Book 15 of the *Iliad*. The 'deceitful bow' is thus a forceful image of dangerous unreliability (cp. Ps. 78: 57). *they relapse into the worship of their high god:* the Hebrew is certainly obscure, as the note states, but the reconstruction, 'they turn to Baal', is simpler and makes excellent sense. ✻

Chapter 8 is again composed of short oracles, some linked by catchwords. Five distinct subjects can be isolated: covenant-breaking, images, political manoeuvring, sacrifices, and buildings.

[a] they relapse...god: *prob. rdg.; Heb. obscure.*
[b] *Prob. rdg.; Heb. adds* that is their stammering speech in Egypt.

OMENS

Put the trumpet to your lips!   **8**
A[a] vulture hovers over the sanctuary of the LORD:
   they have broken my covenant
   and rebelled against my instruction.
They cry to me for help: 2
'We know thee, God of Israel.'[b]
But Israel is utterly loathsome;   3
   and therefore he shall run before the enemy.
They make kings, but not by my will;   4
   they set up officers, but without my knowledge;
they have made themselves idols of their silver and gold.[c]

✳ The cryptic, exclamatory style of the original is partly masked by the N.E.B. translation. 'To your lips the trumpet! A vulture over the Lord's house' (or '*like* a vulture'). This is just the way a prophet might express himself when in a trance state.

  1. *Put the trumpet to your lips!* The prophet sees himself as a watchman, roused to frantic excitement as he catches sight of the enemy. The *vulture* hovering *over the sanctuary* is an omen, which the prophet might have seen either in fact or in vision. The expression '*like* a vulture...' or 'as it were a vulture...' (see the N.E.B. note) suggests visionary experience. What the watchman announces and the omen foreshadows is the coming of the Assyrian armies. *They have broken my covenant and rebelled against my instruction* is no longer part of the oracular speech. It is the kind of rational comment which the prophet offers as explanation of his ecstatic utterance. *Instruction* is the word traditionally rendered in transla-

[a] Prob. rdg.; Heb. Like a.
[b] We...Israel: prob. rdg.; Heb. O my God, we know thee, Israel.
[c] Prob. rdg.; Heb. adds so that he may be cut off.

tions of the Old Testament as 'law'. The traditional rendering is in some ways peculiarly misleading.

2. Although Israel have thus abrogated the covenant with God they go on appealing to him as if it were still intact. '*We know thee, God of Israel.*' In Hosea's view this is the exact opposite of the truth. This is an important indication of the real issue between the prophets and their hearers. The prophets appeal for faithfulness to God, but the people are convinced that they *are* being faithful. The people reject the criteria by which the prophets are judging them.

4. It is uncertain whether verse 4 should be taken with what precedes or with what follows. *They have made themselves idols...* introduces the subject of the next oracle. *They make kings, but not by my will* may refer primarily to contemporary events, in which king ousted king in sharp and disorderly succession, or it may be a comment on the entire past history of the northern monarchy, or even on the institution of the monarchy as such. See notes on 1: 4, 1: 11, 3: 4-5, 9: 9, 10: 9-10, and 13: 9-10. The N.E.B.'s *they make kings...* (present tense) favours the reference to contemporary events, but the Hebrew verbs could equally readily be translated as past. ✳

ON BOVINE GODS

5   Your calf-gods stink,*a* O Samaria;
    my anger flares up against them.
    Long will it be before they prove innocent.
6   For what sort of a god is this bull?
      It is no god,
    a craftsman made it;
    the calf of Samaria will be broken in fragments.

✳ 5. *Your calf-gods stink, O Samaria:* there is no suggestion anywhere else in the Old Testament that there were calf

[a] stink: *or, as otherwise read,* I loathe.

images in Samaria. The calves originally set up by Jeroboam I were in Bethel and Dan. But at that time Samaria had not been built. It would not be surprising if an image had been set up there when it became the capital of the kingdom. *Calf-gods* may be a derogatory term, though this is not certain. Possibly they were meant to represent bulls. Some have suggested that the bull or calf images were originally not idolatrous. In other lands the images of gods stood on pedestals in bovine or other animal shapes. Israel, it is claimed, set up pedestals in her sanctuaries without any image on top. If this was so it would have been a striking demonstration of her devotion to an imageless God, but the theory cannot be proved. In any case, the popular mind seems quickly to have identified the images not as pedestals but as representations of the deity himself.

6. *For what sort of god is this bull?* the Hebrew reads, 'For who is Israel?', which obviously requires emendation of some sort. The N.E.B. translation is based on a clever reconstruction of the text. *It is no god, a craftsman made it:* if Hosea actually said this it is a very early example of this type of argument against idolatry. It is also a very superficial argument, since it assumes that the idolater equates the image with the god. The idolater was no more likely to equate his image with his god than the Christian to equate his crucifix with Christ (see also 13: 2). *.

FUTILE POLICIES

Israel sows the wind and reaps the whirlwind;   7
there are no heads on the standing corn, it yields no
      grain;
and, if it yielded any, strangers would swallow it up.
    Israel is now swallowed up,   8
  lost among the nations,
    a worthless nothing.

9   For, like a wild ass that has left the herd,
        they have run to Assyria.
    Ephraim has bargained for lovers;
10   and, because they have bargained among the nations,
        I will now round them up,
    and then they will soon abandon
        this setting up of kings and[a] princes.

✳ 7. *Israel sows the wind and reaps the whirlwind* seems to be
a proverbial saying. *There are no heads on the standing corn, it
yields no grain* is identified by some as a proverb too. In the
Hebrew it is certainly rhythmical, and, which is rarer, in
rhyme. We might roughly reproduce it as 'Stalk without
head will never make bread'. Together these proverbs would
be a comment on the futility of Israel's policies.

Verse 8 is an explanation of the cryptic verse 7, taking as its
cue the word 'swallow up'. It may be the explanation of an
editor, writing after 722 B.C., when the Assyrians captured
Samaria and deported many of its inhabitants. It is difficult
to see what could otherwise be meant by *Israel is now swallowed
up, lost among the nations*.

Verses 9 and 10 are still on the subject of foreign policy.
It is not clear what the image of the wild ass is meant to convey. Either Israel is pictured as a 'rogue' animal, wilful and
intractable even among its own species, or she is the stray
animal, separated from the herd and very vulnerable to
predators.

9. *they have run to Assyria:* king Hoshea, when he came to
the throne, seems to have appealed to Assyria for assistance
against his opponents within Israel. Menahem likewise tried
to buy Assyrian support (cp. 5: 13). *Ephraim has bargained for
lovers:* a disconcerting change of metaphor, in the Hebrew
manner. Israel is no longer the wild ass, but Israel the prosti-

[a] and: *so Sept.; Heb. om.*

tute, and a prostitute so undesirable that she is no longer sought by her customers, but must go touting for trade.

10. Apart from the first line this verse is obscure in the extreme. The N.E.B. probably represents the best sense that can be got out of it, but we cannot be sure that it is the meaning the writer intended. ✲

TOO MUCH RELIGION

For Ephraim in his sin has multiplied altars,   11
altars have become his sin.
Though I give him countless rules in writing,   12
they are treated as invalid.
Though they sacrifice flesh as offerings to me and eat 13
them,
I,[a] the LORD, will not accept them.
Their guilt will be remembered
and their sins punished.
They shall go back to Egypt,
or in Assyria they shall eat unclean food.[b]

✲ 11. *altars have become his sin:* the altars which were set up in order that sin might be expiated are themselves an occasion for sinful activities.

12. *Though I give him countless rules in writing, they are treated as invalid:* rather than rely on the abundance of his places of worship (Israel *has multiplied altars*), the devotee should pay attention to God's abundant instructions. The text is an interesting witness to the existence of written codes of law.

13. *Their guilt will be remembered:* expiatory offerings were accompanied by prayers that God would 'not remember' the sin. The offerings will be unacceptable and the sins still stand.

[a] *Prob. rdg.; Heb.* he.
[b] or…food: *so Sept.; Heb. om. (cp. 9: 3).*

Sacrifices were part of early Israelite religion, but they seem to have been neither very prominent nor very frequent. After the settlement, and under Canaanite influence, the sacrificial system became progressively more elaborate. It is this elaboration which Hosea seems to be criticizing here. There is nothing in these verses to suggest that he was opposed to sacrifice as such.

They shall go back to Egypt: the most comprehensive punishment of all. God will leave Israel where they were before the history of salvation ever started. It will be as if he had never chosen them and made no covenant, and all his dealings with them and affection for them will go for nothing. *or in Assyria they shall eat unclean food:* added by the N.E.B. from 9: 3. It does not belong here and spoils the climax of the oracle. ✶

DOWN WITH THE CITY!

14   Israel has forgotten his Maker
           and built palaces,
     Judah has multiplied walled cities;
           but I will set fire to his cities,
           and it shall devour his castles.

✶ 14. The word translated *palaces* can equally well mean 'temples'. The verse expresses a point of view which was very ancient in Israel, that for the nation to settle and to build permanent shrines and fortifications was itself an act of apostasy, or at least, that this point of settlement was where the rot set in for Israel. This view was held in highly reactionary circles, with which Amos may have been in touch. *I will set fire to his cities, and it shall devour his castles* is strongly reminiscent of Amos' language. Both Amos and the originator of this verse derive their language from the same circles. It is unlikely that Hosea expressed the sentiments here uttered. The verse has been inserted alongside verses 11–13 which are also critical of the sacrificial system. ✶

Chapter 9 is a collection of oracles concerned with a small cycle of recurring themes. The oracles of verses 1–9 demand a festal setting and were probably delivered at the Autumn Festival at one of the northern sanctuaries.

MISPLACED CELEBRATIONS

Do not rejoice, Israel, do not exult*a* like other peoples; **9**
   for like a wanton you have forsaken your God,
     you have loved an idol*b*
   on every threshing-floor heaped with corn.
Threshing-floor and winepress shall know*c* them no **2**
     more,
     new wine shall disown*d* them.
   They shall not dwell in the LORD's land; **3**
Ephraim shall go back to Egypt,
   or in Assyria they shall eat unclean food.
They shall pour out no wine to the LORD, **4**
they shall not bring their sacrifices to him;
   that would be mourners' fare for them,
   and all who ate it would be polluted.
   For their food shall only stay their hunger;
   it shall not be offered in the house of the LORD.

✻ Like Amos, Hosea appears in the midst of rejoicing and tells the congregation they have nothing to rejoice about. But whereas Amos was inclined to look on the festal ritual as an expression of a corrupt Yahwism, Hosea denies that it is Yahwism at all. It is nothing but Baal-worship.

1. The *threshing-floor* was an open, flat space, ideal for

[a] do not exult: *so Sept.; Heb.* to exultation.
[b] an idol: *or* a harlot's fee.
[c] *So Sept.; Heb.* feed.   [d] *Or* fail.

communal activities, and very appropriate for a harvest celebration. On the use of a threshing-floor for religious purposes see 2 Sam. 24.

2. But the harvest will not last, and the fertility which the rites are designed to stimulate will not be forthcoming much longer, for *threshing-floor and winepress shall know them no more*. The Hebrew actually reads, 'shall feed them no more' (cp. N.E.B. note), a simpler and preferable reading. For *winepress* the Hebrew is simply 'press': the same apparatus was used for pressing olives, an important part of the harvest.

3. On the return to Egypt see the comment on 8: 13. Food eaten in Assyria would be *unclean food* because it would not have been sanctified by the offering of part of it *in the house of the LORD*. In a foreign land, cut off from their own sanctuaries, there will be no more harvest rejoicings with their offerings of firstfruits.

4. *They shall pour out no wine to the LORD, they shall not bring their sacrifices to him*: such offerings would be invalid on foreign soil. Their food will no longer have any sacramental quality, but will serve only the mundane purpose of keeping body and soul together. ✶

THE FATE IN STORE FOR ISRAEL

5   What will you do for the festal day,
        the day of the LORD's pilgrim-feast?
6   For look, they have fled from a scene of devastation:
        Egypt shall receive them,
        Memphis shall be their grave;
        the sands of Syrtes shall wreck them,
        weeds shall inherit their land,
        thorns shall grow in their dwellings.
7   The days of punishment are come,
        the days of vengeance are come
        when Israel shall be humbled.

Then the prophet shall be made a fool
and the inspired seer a madman
by your great guilt.
With great enmity Ephraim lies in wait for God's   8
        people
while the prophet is a fowler's trap by all their paths,
        a snare in the very temple of God.
They lead them deep into sin as at the time of Gibeah. 9
Their guilt will be remembered and their sins punished.

* The same question is put: how will the Israelites manage
for festivals when they are refugees in a foreign land? But now
it is an Egyptian exile that is in the prophet's mind, not an
Assyrian one. Egypt was an obvious place for refugees to flee
to, and it appears that after the sack of Samaria in 722 B.C.
a number did in fact go there.

6. Prophets were expected at festivals to proclaim oracles
of salvation. Like Amos before him, Hosea shocks his audience
by doing the reverse. He looks on the turbulent scene around
him and it is transformed in his visionary imagination into
a scene of devastation. The sands of Syrtes shall wreck them is based
on an emendation of an impossible Hebrew phrase, 'the de-
sirable things of their silver'. An easier emendation is 'Tahpanhes shall mourn them' (Tahpanhes being a coastal town
near the eastern corner of the Nile delta). This provides a better
parallel to the preceding line. The Syrtes are rather a long way
from Egypt, on the coast of what is now Libya and Tunisia,
and the name of another Egyptian city to match Memphis is
what is really required.

7. *Then the prophet shall be made a fool:* when a prophet
prophesied judgement and disaster he was inevitably exposed
to the objection, 'Why should we believe you, when the rest
of our prophets go on predicting salvation?' He could aptly
reply, as Hosea does here, that the befuddling of the prophets

was part of the judgement on the nation. The people themselves had corrupted prophecy by their *great guilt*, so that their
inspired men were no longer capable of giving them warning.

8. Both translation and interpretation of verse 8 are problematical. The first line might plausibly be translated, 'The
prophet is the watchman of Ephraim with my God', or,
emending the Hebrew a little further, '...the watchman of
Ephraim, the people of God'. Either is preferable to the
N.E.B., since it is difficult to see in what sense Ephraim can
be said to lie *in wait for God's people*. The rest of the verse,
accepting the N.E.B.'s rendering, continues to describe how
the prophets, who ought to be acting as the people's watch-
men against disaster, have actually become agents of disaster
themselves.

9. *as at the time of Gibeah*: another example of Hosea's cryptic
use of place-names to recall events. But what event is he recalling? It might refer to the reign of Saul, since Gibeah was
his administrative centre. This would imply that the original
setting up of the monarchy was an act of apostasy. See note on
3: 5. Or it might refer to the atrocity recorded in Judg. 19–21,
the appalling rape and murder of the Levite's concubine at
Gibeah, and the no less appalling vengeance for the crime
(cp. 10: 9–10). *Their guilt will be remembered and their sins
punished* is probably repeated in error from 8: 13. ✻

NO GLORY

10   I came upon Israel like grapes in the wilderness,
        I looked on their forefathers
        with joy like the first ripe figs;
        but they resorted to Baal-peor
        and consecrated themselves to a thing of shame,
11   and Ephraim became as loathsome as the thing he
            loved.
        Their honour shall fly away like a bird:

　　no childbirth, no fruitful womb, no conceiving;
　　even if they rear their children,　　　　　　　　　　12
　　　I will make them childless, without posterity.
　Woe to them indeed when I turn away from them!

✻ This oracle refers back once more to the covenant-making
in the wilderness and the history of Israel's relations with God.
But it recalls it only to show how love went sour.

　10. *like grapes in the wilderness:* grapes do not grow in the
wilderness. The image conveys the miraculous unexpected-
ness of the pleasure. *I looked on their forefathers with joy like the
first ripe figs:* the first fruits of a new season always seem to
taste better than any subsequent ones. The Old Testament
elsewhere uses this image of the eagerness with which the early
figs are seized on. The intensity and rarity of the pleasure
makes the disappointment all the more intense when the let-
down comes. *they resorted to Baal-peor:* i.e. to the baal *of* Peor.
The reference is to Num. 25: 1–5.

　11. *Their honour shall fly away like a bird:* an oblique reference to the loss of the presence of God. The word translated
'honour' is sometimes used of the 'glory' of God's presence,
or even of the ark, the symbol of that presence. Possibly Hosea
is still thinking in terms of the festal ritual, for the pilgrim
came up to the great feast with two expectations, that God
would appear, the glory of the Lord be revealed, and that
fertility would be bestowed. Having dismissed the hope of
God's presence Hosea proceeds to dismiss the other hope also.
There is to be no fertility, *no childbirth, no fruitful womb, no
conceiving.*

　12. The two themes are linked again. No fertility, for *I will
make them childless.* No presence, for I will *turn away from
them.* ✻

TWO SNATCHES OF ORACLES

13 As lion-cubs emerge only to be hunted,[a]
     so must Ephraim bring out his children for slaughter.
14   Give them, O LORD – what wilt thou give them?
     Give them a womb that miscarries and dry breasts.

* 13. Some see this verse as a reference to human sacrifice in
the Baal cult, but this is unnecessary. There is no evidence that
such sacrifice was common, and if it had been, the prophets
would surely have condemned it more frequently and more
explicitly than they do. If the N.E.B. rendering is correct (and
it is as good a guess as any other) the verse would be a brief,
almost proverbial, prophetic saying.

14. The short oracle of verse 14 begins deceptively like an
intercession (*Give them, O LORD...*) but receives a bitter
twist to convert it into an oracle of cursing. *

THE SIN OF GILGAL

15 All their wickedness was seen at Gilgal; there did I hate
          them.
     For their evil deeds I will drive them from my house,
     I will love them no more: all their princes are in revolt.
16   Ephraim is struck down:
     their root is withered, and they yield no fruit;
          if ever they give birth,
     I will slay the dearest offspring of their womb.

17   My God shall reject them,
          because they have not listened to him,
     and they shall become wanderers among the nations.

[a] As lion-cubs...hunted: *prob. rdg.; Heb. unintelligible.*

✻ 15. *All their wickedness was seen at Gilgal:* Gilgal was the place where Saul was proclaimed king. Cp. the note on Gibeah in 9: 9. But this may not be what Hosea means. There may be a hint in 4: 15 that Gilgal was a centre of Baal worship. On its location see the note on Amos 4: 4. *All their princes are in revolt* contains a Hebrew pun which the N.E.B. translators have refrained from trying to reproduce.

17. *They shall become wanderers,* as they were before they settled in the promised land, before the covenant was ever made. Is Hosea thinking of the fact that Gilgal was the first place at which Israel encamped and worshipped after entering Palestine (Josh. 4–5)? This prophecy was fulfilled. After the fall of Samaria in 722 B.C. the northern Israelites were dispersed *among the nations* and the scattered communities eventually lost their identity. ✻

God's judgement on Israel

OF KINGS AND SHRINES

Israel is like a rank vine   **10**
    ripening its fruit:
his fruit grows more and more, and more and more his
        altars;
the fairer his land becomes, the fairer he makes his
        sacred pillars.
They are crazy now, they are mad.   2
    God himself[a] will hack down their altars
        and wreck their sacred pillars,
Well may they say, 'We have no king,   3
    for we do not fear the LORD;
    and what can the king do for us?'

[a] God himself: *lit.* He.

4   There is nothing but talk,
       imposing of oaths and making of treaties, all to no
              purpose;
          and litigation spreads like a poisonous weed
              along the furrows of the fields.
5 The inhabitants of Samaria tremble for the calf-god of
              Beth-aven;
       the people mourn over it*a* and its priestlings howl,
              distressed for their image, their glory,
              which is carried away into exile.
6   It shall be carried to Assyria
          as tribute to the Great King;
       disgrace shall overtake Ephraim
       and Israel shall feel the shame of their disobedience.
7   Samaria and*b* her king are swept away
          like flotsam on the water;
8   the hill-shrines of Aven are wiped out,
          the shrines where Israel sinned;
       thorns and thistles grow over her altars.
          So they will say to the mountains, 'Cover us',
          and to the hills, 'Fall on us.'

✴ This is a collection of oracular material united by its
common concern with altars, shrines and kings.

1. *Israel is like a rank vine:* the image of Israel the vine is
common in the Old Testament. According to the N.E.B. here
the image is that of an unfruitful, unsatisfactory vine. But
the translation 'rank' is debatable. Some would render in
exactly the opposite sense, 'luxuriant'. But the prophet's main
contention is clear, that the fruits of Israel's success have been
spent on apostasy, on more lavish sanctuaries and altars to Baal.

[a] the people mourn over it: *or* the high god and his people mourn.
[b] and: *prob. rdg., cp. Targ.; Heb. om.*

3. *'We have no king'* may well have been spoken by the
people after the assassination of Pekah, before the issue of the
succession was settled. The prophet sees it as ironic. It spoke
more truth than the people were aware, for they had aban-
doned the only true king of Israel, God himself.

4. *There is nothing but talk. . .* may be referring specifically
to the rituals in which a king entered into a covenant at his
coronation and renewed it year by year; a covenant to uphold
justice and to serve God and his people. It is all mere words,
says Hosea, *nothing but talk*, this oath-taking and covenant-
making, for in practice justice is rank, and kings do nothing
to set matters right.

Verses 5–8 are a prophecy of the judgement that will overtake the shrines and altars.

5. *priestlings:* not the normal Hebrew word for 'priests',
but one usually reserved for the ministers of heathen gods. In
applying it to the priests of an Israelite shrine Hosea is im-
plicitly condemning its worship as apostate.

6. *It shall be carried to Assyria:* it was customary when cities
were conquered for their gods to be taken off as spoil, partly
to demonstrate the victory of the conqueror over his opponents' divinities, partly for the sake of the precious metal of
which they were composed. *The Great King* is a title by which
Assyrian emperors were commonly known. ✳

THE DAY OF GIBEAH

Since the day of Gibeah Israel has sinned;   9
  there they took their stand in rebellion.*[a]*
Shall not war overtake them in Gibeah?
I have come*[b]* against the rebels to chastise them,   10
and the peoples shall mass against them
  in hordes for their two deeds of shame.

[a] in rebellion: *so Targ.; Heb. om.*
[b] I have come: *prob. rdg., cp. Sept.; Heb.* By my desire.

✵ On *Gibeah* see the notes on 9: 9. The reference to *their two deeds of shame* (verse 10) may indicate that Hosea has in mind here both the setting up of Saul as king and the earlier atrocity of Judg. 19–21. ✵

SOME AGRICULTURAL IMAGES

11   Ephraim is like a heifer broken in,
        which loves to thresh corn,
    across whose fair neck I have laid a yoke;[a]
     I have harnessed Ephraim to the pole that he[b] may
        plough,
     that Jacob may harrow his land.
12   Sow for yourselves in justice,
        and you will reap what loyalty deserves.
     Break up your fallow;
        for[c] it is time to seek the LORD,
    seeking him till he comes and gives you just measure
        of rain.
13 *a*   You have ploughed wickedness into your soil,
        and the crop is mischief;
        you have eaten the fruit of treachery.

✵ These verses constitute a pair of short oracles having nothing in common except that their images are drawn from agriculture.

11. *a heifer...which loves to thresh corn:* what is in mind is not the pulling of a threshing sledge (see note on Amos 1: 3) but the other method of threshing, in which the animal merely walked round and round, beating out the corn by trampling. This was easy work, and moreover, if the law of Deut. 25: 4

[a] a yoke: *prob. rdg.; Heb. om.*
[b] he: *prob. rdg.; Heb.* Judah.   [c] *So Pesh.; Heb.* and.

was in force at this time, the animal was allowed to eat as it worked. Israel is like a draught animal which finds such labour congenial but objects to the less rewarding toil of ploughing and harrowing.

12. *Sow for yourselves in justice, and you will reap what loyalty deserves* is a saying of proverbial type.

13. *You have ploughed wickedness into your soil...* is the prophet's assertion that the people have disregarded this ancient wisdom. They will now reap what they have sown. *

AN ATTACK ON ISRAEL

Because you have trusted in your chariots,[a]   13 *b*
    in the number of your warriors,
the tumult of war shall arise against your people,   14
    and all your fortresses shall be razed
as Shalman razed Beth-arbel in the day of battle,
    dashing the mother to the ground with her babes.
So it shall be done to you, Bethel,[b]   15
    because of your evil scheming;
as sure as day dawns, the king of Israel shall be swept
    away.

* A complete change of subject. Here it is Israel's trust in military strength that is criticized.

14. The incident referred to in the words *as Shalman razed Beth-arbel in the day of battle* cannot with certainty be identified, though a number of attempts to do so have been made.

15. The translation, *as sure as day dawns*, takes some liberties with the text. 'At dawn' is the literal rendering. This might mean, 'when the battle has barely begun'. Some scholars prefer to read a very similar word and translate 'in the storm'.

[a] chariots: *so Sept.; Heb.* way.
[b] Bethel: *or, with Sept.,* house of Israel.

Otherwise 'dawn' might be intended as a synonym for 'the hour of deliverance', as it seems to be in Ps. 46: 5. The prophet would then be saying, 'At the very hour when deliverance is due, disaster will strike.' But perhaps the best suggestion is that we should read not 'at dawn' but 'in the gate' (*bash-sha'ar* instead of *bash-shahar*). The reference would then be to the conqueror's setting up his throne in the city gateway (the normal place for public assembly) and dispensing to his captives their deserts. A scene of this sort is described in Jer. 39: 3. *

Hos. 11: 1-9 is a little discourse on the theme of Israel as the son of God. Into it has been inserted verses 5-7, on quite a different subject.

THE PRODIGAL SON

The Patient Father?

11   When Israel was a boy, I loved him;
    I called my son out of Egypt;
2   but the more I[a] called, the further they went from me;[b]
    they must needs sacrifice to the Baalim
        and burn offerings before carved images.
3   It was I who taught Ephraim to walk,
    I who had taken[c] them in my[d] arms;
4   but they did not know that I harnessed them in leading-
            strings[e]
    and led them with bonds of love[f] –
    that I had lifted them like a little child[g] to my cheek,
    that I had bent down to feed them.

[a] So Sept.; Heb. they.   [b] So Sept.; Heb. them.
[c] I who had taken: so Sept.; Heb. unintelligible.
[d] So Sept.; Heb. his.
[e] leading-strings: or cords of leather.
[f] bonds of love: or reins of hide.
[g] I had...child: prob. rdg.; Heb. like those who lift up a yoke.

✻ The idea of the fatherhood of God, contrary to popular belief, is neither peculiarly Christian nor peculiarly biblical. The Baal-worshippers of Hosea's time were very familiar with the notion. Their high god, El, is father of the gods and is commonly entitled in the Canaanite texts, 'Father of Men'.

1. *When Israel was a boy...*: when in the Old Testament Israel is described as God's child it is sometimes as 'son' and sometimes as 'daughter'. *I called my son out of Egypt*: it was the event of the exodus that first made Israel conscious of his sonship, but from early times he has been recalcitrant, and at best unresponsive.

3–4. The disappointed father looks back to the days when the child was young and dependent on him. *It was I who taught Ephraim to walk*: in the N.E.B. verse 4 is taken as an extension of the same metaphor. As the text stands in Hebrew it reads, 'But they did not know that it was I who healed them.' *That I harnessed them in leading-strings* is based on an attractive re-interpretation, and one that fits the context well. The suggestion in the N.E.B. note, 'reins of hide' instead of *bonds of love*, turns on the fact that the words 'love' and 'hide' are identical. The prophet may be making a deliberate play on words and expect his hearers to understand both meanings. The rest of verse 4 is obscure but the reading opted for by the N.E.B. is again an attractive one in the context. ✻

A WARLIKE INTERLUDE

Back they shall go to Egypt,   5
the Assyrian shall be their king;
   for they have refused to return to me.
The sword shall be swung over their blood-spattered 6
    altars
   and put an end to their prattling priests
and devour my people in return for all their   7
    schemings,

bent on rebellion as they are.
Though they call on their high god,
    even then he will not reinstate them.

✷ These verses deal with the punishment of the nation by war and their deportation or flight to Egypt and Assyria.

5. *Back they shall go to Egypt:* on the return to Egypt see the comment on 8: 13.

6. The word translated *prattling priests* is a dubious one and a number of alternative suggestions has been made. ✷

THE PARABLE RESUMED

8 How can I give you up, Ephraim,
        how surrender you, Israel?
   How can I make you like Admah
        or treat you as Zeboyim?
   My heart is changed within me,
        my remorse kindles already.
   I will not let loose my fury,
9   I will not turn round and destroy Ephraim;
   for I am God and not a man,
        the Holy One in your midst;

✷ The background to the prophet's thinking here is to be found in Deut. 21: 18–21, the law of the rebellious son. This law lays down the death penalty for delinquent children, if the parents submit the case to the court of elders. We do not know how often, if at all, this ferocious law was appealed to. Could any parent really have brought himself to invoke it? Hosea shares our horror at the thought. *How can I give you up, Ephraim...?* (verse 8).

8. *Admah* and *Zeboyim* cannot be identified, and about the circumstances of their overthrow nothing is known. We only

know that they are sometimes linked in scripture with Sodom and Gomorrah as proverbial instances of total and spectacular destruction. *My heart is changed...*: the heart, in the view of the ancient Israelites, was not the seat of the emotions, but of thought and will. The seat of the emotions was in the bowels.

The Old Testament thinks of God largely in terms of two different and alternative images, as king, or as father. When he is thought of primarily as king, as the upholder of law, it is his justice which receives emphasis. It is unthinkable that he should be anything but unshakably righteous, allowing no deviation from his just demands. But when he is conceived as father it seems unthinkable that he should be anything other than compassionate. Christianity has brought the two images firmly together, with all the inevitable paradox and tension that this involves, for we habitually pray, 'Our *Father* ...thy *kingdom* come'.

9. Hosea now does something very characteristic of the Old Testament writers. Having talked of God in terms of intensely human analogies (and Hosea exploits such analogies with a mastery that few religious minds before or since have rivalled), he puts all analogy in its place with a single, shattering statement: *for I am God and not a man, the Holy One in your midst.* However useful the analogy of human love may be, it fails to convey everything that needs to be conveyed. For in the last resort God's love is *un*like human love. Human love does have its limits. Marriages do sometimes end in divorce and parents do sometimes take their delinquent children before the courts. The love of God, Hosea implies, has no such limits. The title *Holy One* indicates the total difference of God from men. ✵

ISRAEL, ASSYRIA AND EGYPT

10   I will not come with threats[a] like a roaring lion.
          No; when I roar, I who am God,[b]
      my sons shall come with speed out of the west.

11   They will come speedily, flying like birds out of
          Egypt,
          like pigeons from Assyria,
      and I will settle them in their own homes.
      This is the very word of the LORD.

12[c] Ephraim besets me with treachery,
          the house of Israel besets me with deceit;
      and Judah is still restive under God,
          still loyal to the idols he counts holy.

12   Ephraim is a shepherd whose flock is but[d] wind,
      a hunter chasing the east wind all day;[e]
      he makes a treaty with Assyria
      and carries tribute of oil to Egypt.

* Here we have a collection of oracular material, some of it
definitely later than Hosea's time, on the theme of Israel's
relations with Egypt and Assyria. Verses 10–11, speaking of
the return of Israelite captives from Assyria and refugees from
Egypt, manifestly comes from a period after the fall of Samaria
in 722 B.C.

12. It is odd to find Judah mentioned here at all, and difficult to decide what the statement about her originally meant.
As the Hebrew text stands it seems to contrast Judah favour-
ably with Israel. 'Judah still roams with God, is faithful to the

[a] *Prob. rdg.; Heb. adds* they shall go after the LORD.
[b] God: *lit.* He.   [c] *12: 1 in Heb.*
[d] is a...but: *or* feeds on.
[e] *Prob. rdg.; Heb. adds* piling up treachery and havoc.

140

Holy One.' But the word 'roams' is an odd one and excites
suspicion, and the N.E.B. is probably correct in emending
the text to make it unfavourable. It is possible that verse 12
was originally a genuine oracle of Hosea's, relating to Israel,
and that a later hand has both inserted the reference to Judah
and converted the second line into an expression of approval.

12: 1. On Israel's political relations with Assyria and Egypt
see note on 7: 11. ✳

We may perhaps take chapters 12–13 as a connected whole, a
meditation on the history of Israel's relations with God. It
begins with the career of Jacob, and then, in less detail, refers
to the exodus and settlement traditions, the wanderings, unfaithfulness during the period of the judges, the setting up of
the monarchy, and finally comes down to Hosea's own day.
The object of the survey is to show that Israel's apostasy is
entirely in character. The historical traditions are not precisely
in the chronological order which we should expect. Either
Hosea is not attempting a chronologically ordered exposition
or else he has received the traditions in a different order from
that embodied in the Pentateuch.

But in any case, the passage is not a tightly organized commentary on the history. The thought flits from one incident
to another, without clearly logical connections always being
established between them. And furthermore, into the trace-
able outline is inserted material which is difficult to relate to
the main theme of the passage. We may conclude that if it
ever was more tightly organized, a good deal of extraneous
matter has been inserted into it.

THE RASCAL JACOB

The LORD has a charge to bring against Judah   2
and is resolved to punish Jacob for his conduct;
    he will requite him for his misdeeds.
    Even in the womb Jacob overreached his brother,   3

and in manhood he strove with God.

4   The divine angel stood firm and held his own;[a]
Jacob wept and begged favour for himself.
        Then God met him at Bethel
and there spoke with him.[b]

5   The LORD the God of Hosts, the LORD is his name.

✻ 2. *The LORD has a charge to bring*...: the prophet models his indictment on the speech used by a prosecuting counsel in a court of law. *against Judah:* this is unexpected. The accusation concerns itself exclusively with Jacob/Israel. There can be little doubt that the words were originally addressed to Israel and that after the book of Hosea was taken over by the religious community in the south the word 'Judah' was inserted to make it more relevant to their needs.

3. In the book of Genesis *Jacob* is an ambiguous character. He is divinely blessed, yet he does not always appear to deserve it. In what light does Hosea regard him? The question can be answered in different ways, according to how we choose to translate some of the problematic verses which follow. But verse 2, which says that *the LORD...is resolved to punish Jacob for his conduct* and *requite him for his misdeeds*, seems to establish unmistakably that Hosea looks on Jacob's conduct as reprehensible, and we are entitled to look for an interpretation of the following verses which fits in with this view. *Jacob overreached his brother* refers to the events of Gen. 25: 6. The verb *overreach* makes a pun on the name 'Jacob', a pun which appears in Gen. 25. *He strove* is a pun on Jacob's other name, Israel. A similar one occurs in Gen. 32: 28, in a description of the wrestling at Jabbok, which Hosea goes on to refer to in verse 4.

4. *The divine angel stood firm and held his own:* the Hebrew is ambiguous, as the N.E.B. note makes clear. It is not certain

[a] The divine...own: *or* He stood firm against an angel, but flagged.
[b] *So Sept.; Heb.* us.

whether Jacob or the angel is the subject of the verbs, and it is
not certain whether the second verb means 'to hold one's own'
or 'to flag'. Hosea's words are strongly reminiscent of the
statement about Jacob in Gen. 32: 28, that Jacob 'strove with
God and with men, and prevailed'. Hosea is evidently referring
to the same tradition (though he did not, of course, know the
book of Genesis in its present form), and the Genesis statement
should probably be allowed to determine the meaning here.
In this case a reading should be preferred which is that neither
of the N.E.B. text nor its footnote: 'He stood firm against an
angel, and held his own.' It is sometimes objected that if
Hosea means that Jacob held his own against the angel he
would hardly go on to say that he *wept and begged favour* of his
adversary. It is true that this seems inconsistent, but the in-
consistency is there already in the Genesis tradition, which
asserts both that Jacob 'prevailed' and also that he entreated
his adversary to bless him.

But even the rascally Jacob had in the end to come to terms
with God. In verse 6 the moral is pointed: 'Turn back all
of you.' *

ISRAEL IN CANAAN

Turn back all of you by God's help;   6
practise loyalty and justice
and wait always upon your God.
False scales are in merchants' hands,   7
    and they love to cheat;
        so Ephraim says,   8
'Surely I have become a rich man, I have made my
            fortune';
    but all his*a* gains will not pay
        for the guilt*b* of his sins.

[a] *So Sept.; Heb.* my.
[b] for the guilt: *prob. rdg.; Heb.* for me, guilt.

9   Yet I have been the LORD your God since your days in
      Egypt;

     I will make you live in tents yet again, as in the old
      days.

✶ 7-8. The word *cana' an* in Hebrew means both 'Canaanite'
and 'merchant'. So in *false scales are in merchants' hands* the
word-play is probably intentional. Israel, once in Canaan,
took to Canaanite ways, to trade and sharp practice, and became an affluent society. But all his affluence *will not pay for the
guilt of his sins*.

There is another piece of word-play which runs through
this passage. The Hebrew word *'on* has already appeared in
verse 3, where the N.E.B. translates 'manhood'; in his *'on*
'he strove with God'. In verse 8 it appears as 'fortune': *I have
become a rich man, I have made my 'on*. In verse 11, pronounced
with different vowels, as *'awen*, it means 'idolatry'. *'On*,
'wealth', 'affluence', is what Jacob seeks. *'On*, 'prosperity',
'strength', is what he exults in. But *'awen* (spelled in exactly
the same way in Hebrew) is what he finds: and *'awen* is not
only 'idolatry' but 'trouble' and 'sorrow'.

Whether these groups of verses were linked in this way by
Hosea himself or by someone who collected his oracles, the
play on words brings out the prophet's thought excellently.

9. *Yet I have been the LORD your God since your days in
Egypt:* Hosea seems almost to be willing to write off the
patriarchs (he clearly believes that Jacob got the nation off to
a bad start) and to see the real relationship with God as being
initiated at the exodus. Hosea is not alone in this, for the book
of Deuteronomy seems to share his attitude. *I will make you
live in tents yet again, as in the old days:* these words have sometimes been interpreted as a threat, but this is not in character.
Hosea looks back with nostalgia on the wilderness period as
a kind of honeymoon with God (see 2: 14). This is not a
threat, therefore, but a promise. *As in the old days* could readily

be translated, 'as in the festival'. This would make it a reference to the ritual living in tents at the Autumn Festival, the
Feast of Tabernacles. *

ISRAEL AND ARAM

I spoke to the prophets,   10
it was I who gave vision after vision;
I spoke through the prophets in parables.
Was there idolatry in Gilead?   11
    Yes: they were worthless
and sacrificed to bull-gods in Gilgal;
their altars were common as heaps of stones beside
        a ploughed field.

Jacob fled to the land of Aram;   12
Israel did service to win a wife,
    to win a wife he tended sheep.

By a prophet the LORD brought up Israel out of Egypt 13
    and by a prophet he was tended.

* 11. This is a difficult verse, but two observations may be
made on it. It contains the word *'on* (here translated *idolatry*),
which may be part of the reason for its presence in this passage.
It also stands at the beginning of another brief disquisition on
the life of Jacob, and this may give us the clue to its original
meaning. It may originally have referred to the covenant-
making between Jacob and Laban, his Aramaean (Syrian)
father-in-law (Gen. 31: 46–54). This story involves a 'cairn of
witness' called 'Galeed', which is also referred to as a stone
heap, *gal* in Hebrew. These words may have been corrupted
to *Gilead* and *Gilgal*. The original text would be a condemnation of the Jacob/Laban covenant as a reprehensible act. Just
as the earlier mention of Jacob's overreaching his brother may

have a contemporary reference to Israel's dealings with Judah, so the criticism of Jacob's covenant with Laban would convey condemnation of Israel's coalition with Syria. We have already seen what Hosea thought of this particular piece of power politics (see notes on 5: 8–15).

Verses 12–13 continue this thought, contemptuously referring to Jacob's Syrian bondage for the sake of a woman, and contrasting it with God's redemption of Israel through a prophet.

Hosea's very negative attitude to the Jacob traditions may seem surprising. He does not regard Jacob as a hero at all, and episodes which in Genesis are taken as redounding to Jacob's glory are treated by Hosea with scorn. But there is no reason why different thinkers should not evaluate the same traditions in different ways. Hosea's interpretation surprises us only because we are more familiar with the Genesis presentation of the traditions and therefore regard it as normative. *

EPHRAIM AND HIS IDOLS

14   Ephraim has given bitter provocation;
      therefore his Lord will make him answerable
        for his own death
      and bring down upon his own head the blame
        for all that he has done.

13   When the Ephraimites mumbled their prayers,[a]
      God himself denounced Israel;
      they were guilty of Baal-worship and died.

2   Yet now they sin more and more;
      they have made themselves an image of cast metal,
      they have fashioned[b] their silver into idols,

[a] *Mng. of Heb. uncertain.*
[b] they have fashioned: *so Sept.; Heb. obscure.*

> nothing but the work of craftsmen;
> men say of them,
> 'Those who kiss calf-images offer human sacrifice.'
> Therefore they shall be like the morning mist   3
>   or like dew that vanishes early,
> like chaff blown from the threshing-floor
>   or smoke from a chimney.

✳ 12: 14. The prophet delivers a final judgement before leaving the patriarchal period and moving on to consider subsequent history. He now no longer refers to 'Jacob' but 'Ephraim'. On Ephraim see note on 4: 18.

13: 1. *When the Ephraimites mumbled their prayers...*: a difficult line, as the N.E.B. note indicates. One alternative is to take it as a reference to Ephraim's glorious past: 'When Ephraim spoke, there was trembling...' Ephraim had once been the most important tribe. His idolatry has brought him low.

2. *nothing but the work of craftsmen*: on this kind of polemic see the note on 8: 6. '*Those who kiss calf-images offer human sacrifice*': this is a fair representation of what the Hebrew says, though what it originally meant is another matter. It does not imply that human sacrifice was offered in Hosea's time, but appears to suggest only that idolatry is *as bad as* human sacrifice. ✳

SHEPHERD OR LEOPARD?

> But I have been the Lord your God since your days 4
>   in Egypt,
>   when you knew no other saviour than me,
>   no god but me.
>   I cared for you in the wilderness,   5
> in a land of burning heat, as if you were in pasture. 6
>   So they were filled,

> and, being filled, grew proud;
>   and so they forgot me.
>
> 7 So now I will be[a] like a panther to them,
>   I will prowl like a leopard by the wayside;
>
> 8 I will meet them like a she-bear robbed of her cubs
>   and tear their ribs apart,
>   like a lioness I will devour them on the spot,
>   I will rip them up like a wild beast.

✱ Read verses 7–8 alongside Psalm 23 and you will catch something of the impact the prophet's words must have made on his first hearers, brought up on the traditional ideas about the divine shepherd.

5. I cared for you in the wilderness: God shepherded them, protecting them from ravening beasts. Now he *is* the ravening beast. The shepherd has turned wolf, *panther...leopard...she-bear...lioness...wild beast* (cp. 5: 14). ✱

MONARCHY

> 9 I have destroyed you, O Israel; who[b] is there to help
>   you?
>
> 10 Where now is your king that he may save you,
>   or the rulers in all your cities
>   for whom you asked me,
>   begging for king and princes?
>
> 11 I gave you a king in my anger,
>   and in my fury took him away.

✱ Hosea returns to one of his favourite subjects, the monarchy, making it clear this time that he is not only antagonistic to the

[a] I will be: *so Sept.; Heb.* I was.
[b] who: *so Sept.; Heb.* in me.

northern kings but to monarchy as such. The monarchy is
powerless to save the nation. Israel was wrong to ask for a
king. Her punishment was that she got what she asked. For
more detailed discussion of Hosea's attitude to the monarchy
see the notes on 3 : 5. ✶

THE STILLBORN PEOPLE

Ephraim's guilt is tied up in a scroll,   12
   his sins are kept on record.
When the pangs of his birth came over his mother,   13
   he showed himself a senseless child;
     for at the proper time he could not present himself
     at the mouth of the womb.
     Shall I redeem him from Sheol?   14
Shall I ransom him from death?
Oh, for your plagues, O death! Oh, for your sting,
     Sheol!
I will put compassion out of my sight.
Though he flourishes among the reeds,[a]   15
an east wind shall come, a blast from the LORD,
   rising over the desert;
Ephraim's spring will fail and his fountain run dry.
   It will carry away as spoil
     his whole store of costly treasures.
Samaria will become desolate because she has rebelled 16[b]
     against her God;
her babes will fall by the sword and be dashed to the
     ground,
   her women with child shall be ripped up.

[a] among the reeds: *prob. rdg.; Heb.* between (*or* a son ɔf) brothers.
[b] *14: 1 in Heb.*

* 12. *his sins are kept on record:* an allusion to the records kept by ancient kings of the doings of their vassals. Cp., for example, Ezra 4: 14–19.

13. A sudden change of metaphor. Ephraim is like a baby that cannot be brought to birth, an all too common occurrence in the days when obstetric science was unknown. It might be a reference to an otherwise unrecorded legend about the birth of Ephraim. What the prophet seems to be saying is that there is a possibility of national rebirth and renewal, which the nation is characteristically refusing.

14–15. Another change of imagery. The background to these verses is to be sought in Canaanite mythology. *Death* (Moth) was the proper name of the god of summer and of drought, who was able to defeat even the mighty Baal. Though the nation *flourishes among the reeds*, i.e. in well-watered and therefore fertile places, even there the *east wind*, the dry desert wind, will roast them out. In the myths it is death who wields this withering weapon, but for Hosea the drying wind is the *ruaḥ* ('wind' or 'spirit') of God himself. *Oh, for your plagues, O death!* The traditional rendering of verse 14 (supported by no less than the apostle Paul, cp. 1 Cor. 15: 55) makes it a promise. 'O Death, where is your victory? O Death, where is your sting?' Modern scholarship is virtually unanimous in taking it as a threat. God is summoning up the plagues of death to punish his recalcitrant people. Death, for Hosea, is not an independent power, opposed to the good God, as he was for the Canaanites, but a mere weapon in God's hand.

15. *an east wind shall come...It will carry away as spoil his whole store of costly treasures:* a rapid change of imagery, from the desolation caused by the summer drought to the desolation of war. To the Palestinian mind these two images are closely related. In the Canaanite myths the onset of the summer drought is presented as a battle.

16. *Samaria will become desolate*, or, possibly, 'will bear her guilt'. *

Repentance, forgiveness, and restoration

Chapter 14 falls into three parts. Verses 1–3 are an appeal by the prophet, and an expression of repentance which he puts into the people's mouth. In verses 4–8 we have God's reply, which is probably a composite speech made up of two or three salvation oracles which were originally unrelated, but brought together because they contained the word 'Lebanon'.

This pattern, a prayer of the people followed by answering salvation oracles, may have been the normal order for a public service of penitence. There is evidence that such services were held when circumstances called for them. An editor has presumably put together Hoseanic material in this way for use in such a liturgy.

The third section of the chapter consists simply of verse 9.

AN APPEAL

Return, O Israel, to the LORD your God;   **14**

    for you have stumbled in your evil courses.

  Come with your words ready,   2

    come back to the LORD;

say to him, 'Thou dost not*a* endure iniquity.*b*

    Accept our plea,

  and we will pay our vows with cattle from our 3

    pens.*c*

Assyria shall not save us, nor will we seek horses to ride;

[a] not: *prob. rdg., cp. Sept.; Heb.* all.
[b] Thou…iniquity: *or* Thou wilt surely take away iniquity.
[c] cattle from our pens: *or, as otherwise read,* fruit from our lips.

what we have made with our own hands
we will never again call gods;
for in thee the fatherless find a father's love.'

* This is a sudden change of tune from the oracle at the end of the previous chapter, but it was customary to end a book with favourable words and the compiler is following the usual pattern. 13: 12–16 appeared to deny that Israel any longer has the option of repentance. 14: 1–3 appeals for repentance none the less. This is not a good enough reason for denying that Hosea could have spoken these words. When a prophet formally denies that repentance is of any use he may sometimes be trying merely to bring home the seriousness of the situation. Or, if Hosea really means what he says in chapter 13, the words of chapter 14 may come from a different period in his ministry; either an earlier, more hopeful, one, or a later one, after Assyrian attack had brought Israel to a more penitent frame of mind.

1. *you have stumbled:* the word 'stumble' in modern English conjures up a picture of a man thrown momentarily off balance, of a near-mishap. But in Hebrew it is a much stronger word. 'To stumble' in the bible means 'to come to utter disaster'.

2. '*Thou dost not endure iniquity*': the reading in the N.E.B. note, 'Thou wilt surely take away iniquity', is perhaps preferable. *cattle from our pens:* footnote, 'fruit from our lips'. The uncertainty about the correct translation is especially unfortunate. *Cattle from our pens* implies that Israel's penitence, to be effective, must express itself in the offering of sacrifices. 'Fruit from our lips' suggests just the opposite, that prayer and praise alone are being offered, and that this is all that is needed. If we could be confident that Hosea was radically opposed to sacrifice, as 8: 13 might suggest (and cp. 6: 6), this would be decisive in favour of the reading in the footnote. 'Fruit of the lips' looks like an improbable expression, but a similar phrase, 'fruit of the mouth', occurs twice in the book

of Proverbs, and it is therefore not unlikely to be a genuine Hebrew idiom.

3. *nor will we seek horses:* i.e. cavalry (or chariotry). Israel will no longer trust to the great powers and their armed forces to defend her, but will rely on God. ✻

A PROMISE

I will heal their apostasy; of my own bounty will I love 4
    them;
    for my anger is turned away from them.
I will be as dew to Israel   5
    that he may flower like the lily,
strike root like the poplar[a]
    and put out fresh shoots,   6
that he may be as fair as the olive
    and fragrant as Lebanon.
Israel shall again dwell[b] in my[c] shadow   7
    and grow corn in abundance;
    they shall flourish like a vine
    and be famous as the wine of Lebanon.
What has Ephraim[d] any more to do with idols?   8
    I have spoken and I affirm it:
    I am the pine-tree that shelters you;
    to me you owe your fruit.

✻ 4. *I will heal their apostasy:* 'heal' is an odd word to use of apostasy, but it is a favourite word of Hosea's and obviously very significant for him (cp. 5: 13, 6: 1, 7: 1).

5. *I will be as dew to Israel:* the dew in Palestine is some-

[a] *Prob. rdg.; Heb.* like Lebanon.
[b] *So Sept.; Heb.* dwellers.   [c] *Prob. rdg.; Heb.* its.
[d] What has Ephraim: *so Sept.; Heb.* Ephraim, what have I.

times extremely heavy and is an important source of water for plant life. *lily...poplar...olive...*: the botanical imagery is highly characteristic of Hebrew love poetry. Compare, for example, Song of Songs 2: 1–6.

8. *I am the pine-tree that shelters you:* when a Palestinian talks of shelter he is usually thinking of shelter from the sun, not from the wind and the rain. ✻

A CLOSING COMMENT

9 Let the wise consider these things and let him who considers take note; for the LORD's ways are straight and the righteous walk in them, while sinners stumble.

✻ This closing verse was added by some Jewish scribe long after Hosea's time. It sums up what the scribe took to be the moral of the book. ✻

✻ ✻ ✻ ✻ ✻ ✻ ✻ ✻ ✻ ✻ ✻ ✻ ✻ ✻ ✻

MICAH

✳ ✳ ✳ ✳ ✳ ✳ ✳ ✳ ✳ ✳ ✳ ✳ ✳

SUPERSCRIPTION

T HIS IS THE WORD OF THE LORD which came to **1**
Micah of Moresheth during the reigns of Jotham,
Ahaz, and Hezekiah, kings of Judah; which he received
in visions concerning Samaria and Jerusalem.

✳ *Moresheth:* see on 1: 10. On the date of Micah's activities
see p. 4. Micah is a southerner, but concerns himself
explicitly with both halves of the nation, with *Samaria and
Jerusalem.* ✳

The rulers of Israel and Judah
denounced

Verses 2–9 make up a judgement poem which sets the tone
for this first section of the work, chapters 1–3. (On the structure of the book see pp. 10–11.)

GOD COMES IN JUDGEMENT

Listen, you peoples, all together;   2
attend, O earth and all who are in it,
that the Lord GOD, the Lord from his holy temple,
    may bear witness against you.
For look, the LORD is leaving his dwelling-place;   3
down he comes and walks on the heights of the earth.

4   Beneath him mountains dissolve
        like wax before the fire,
        valleys are torn open,
    as when torrents pour down the hill-side –
5   and all for the crime of Jacob and the sin of Israel.[a]
    What is the crime of Jacob? Is it not Samaria?
    What is the hill-shrine of Judah? Is it not Jerusalem?
6   So I will make Samaria
    a heap of ruins in open country,
        a place for planting vines;
        I will pour her stones down into the valley
        and lay her foundations bare.
7   All her carved figures shall be shattered,
        her images burnt one and all;
        I will make a waste heap of all her idols.
            She amassed them out of fees for harlotry,
            and a harlot's fee shall they become once more.
8   Therefore I must howl and wail,
        go naked and distraught;
    I must howl like a wolf, mourn like a desert-owl.
9   Her wound cannot be healed;
            for the stroke has bitten deep into Judah,
            it has fallen on the gate of my people,
            upon Jerusalem itself.

* The prophet begins in the manner of an accuser in the law court. The accuser customarily opened his accusation by calling on heaven and earth and on God himself to witness to the truth of what he was saying. But the perspective quickly changes. Having at first called on God to *bear witness* (verse 2),

[a] *So Heb.; but possibly read* Judah.

the prophet sees the Lord with the eye of vision coming to inflict punishment.

3. *the LORD is leaving his dwelling-place:* on God's 'place' see the comment on Hos. 5: 15, a passage which makes an interesting contrast with the present one. Micah clearly conceives of God dwelling in heaven, which he would think of as being above the visible sky. *His holy temple,* mentioned in verse 2, is evidently his heavenly, not his earthly, dwelling. Solomon's prayer at the dedication of the temple, 1 Kings 8: 27 (a passage which was not written in the time of Solomon and cannot be earlier than the late seventh century), implies that even to speak of God's dwelling in heaven is to use only a figure of speech.

The description of the appearance of God is to some extent conventional, but manages to be at the same time terrifying. God is conceived as a gigantic figure, striding over *the heights of the earth*, the mountains melting under his feet *like wax before the fire* (verse 4).

5. What has prompted this terrifying visitation? It is *all for the crime of Jacob and the sin of* Judah. The reading 'Judah' (see the N.E.B.'s note) is inherently more probable. The sins of the two nations are epitomized in their two capitals. *What is the crime of Jacob? Is it not Samaria?* The next line should probably be read, with the Septuagint, 'What is the sin of the house of Judah? Is it not Jerusalem?' The text as it stands, *What is the hill-shrine of Judah?*, suggests that Micah's objections to Samaria and Jerusalem are mainly objections to the kind of worship which goes on in them. The much-vaunted sanctuary of the Lord at Jerusalem is no better than a pagan hill-shrine. It is quite possible, however, that the prophet is thinking primarily of the sins of government in the two countries.

6. The threat of Samaria's destruction was evidently uttered by the prophet before 722 B.C. Some scholars have doubted whether Micah delivered any prophecies as early as this and are therefore obliged either to translate the tenses of the verbs

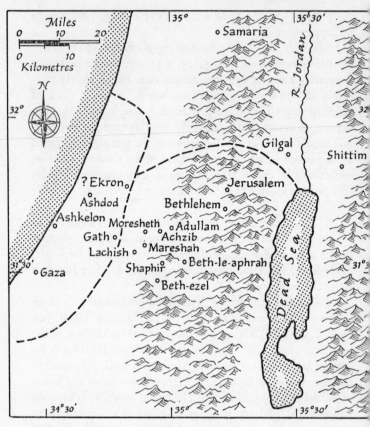

2. Places mentioned particularly in Micah. The location of some of the villages marked is doubtful. The map indicates probable or possible sites only.

differently or to see the passage as a prophecy after the event, inserted at a later date.

7. *She amassed them out of fees for harlotry, and a harlot's fee shall they become once more:* the language is reminiscent of Hosea's. The gold and silver idols, bought from the profits of licentious and heathenish worship, will become spoil to be

offered in the heathen temples of the enemy. This was the
normal fate of idols captured in war.

8. At the prospect of the disaster which he foresees the
prophet breaks into lamentation. *Therefore I must howl and
wail, go naked and distraught:* the behaviour of Isaiah (see Isa.
20) suggests that Micah may not merely be speaking meta-
phorically.

9. Though the prophet has been speaking primarily of the
destruction of Samaria, he envisages the possibility that it may
involve Judah too. Isaiah, speaking apparently just after the
Assyrian sack of Samaria in 722 B.C., thinks in exactly the
same way (Isa. 10: 11). ✳

A LAMENT

The rest of chapter 1 is a poem with several curious features.
It is in the rhythm of the lament, but in content it is a warning
of disaster. It consists of a series of word-plays (quite impossible to reproduce in translation) on place-names. The
places mentioned, insofar as they can be identified, all seem
to be in the same locality, in the strip of country between
Jerusalem and the Philistine border. This is Micah's home
territory.

> Will you not weep your fill, weep your eyes out in 10
>   Gath?
> In Beth-aphrah*ᵃ* sprinkle yourselves with dust;
>   take the road, you that dwell in Shaphir;   11
> have not the people of Zaanan gone out in shame from
>   their city*ᵇ*?
>   Beth-ezel is a place of lamentation,
> she can lend you support no longer.
> The people of Maroth are greatly alarmed,   12

[a] *So Vulg.*; *Heb.* Beth-le-aphrah.
[b] from their city: *prob. rdg.*, *cp. Sept.*; *Heb.* nakedness.

for disaster has come down from the LORD
to the very gate of Jerusalem.

13   Harness the steeds to the chariot, O people of Lachish,
for you first led the daughter of Zion into sin;
to you must the crimes of Israel be traced.

14   Let Moresheth-gath be given her dismissal.
Beth-achzib has[a] disappointed[b] the kings of Israel.

15   And you too, O people of Mareshah,
I will send others to take your place;
and the glory of Israel shall hide in the cave of Adullam.

16   Shave the hair from your head in mourning
for the children of your delight;
make yourself bald as a vulture,
for they have left you and gone into exile.

✻ 10. *Will you not weep your fill, weep your eyes out in Gath?*:
the N.E.B. has restored the text with the help of the Septuagint. The Hebrew actually reads, 'Tell it not in Gath', which
is probably an error by a scribe who was thinking of the
opening of David's lament over Saul in 2 Sam. 1: 20. Gath
was a border town, the nearest of the Philistine cities to Israel.
The name of Micah's own village, Moresheth-gath, suggests
that, though it was an Israelite village, it was close enough to
Gath to be regarded as a satellite of that city. *In Beth-aphrah
sprinkle yourselves with dust*: the Hebrew for 'dust' is *'aphar*.
To sprinkle dust on one's head was a sign of mourning or
distress. Compare, e.g., Josh. 7: 6, where the elders of Israel
throw dust on their heads in distress after the defeat of their
forces at Ai.

11. *take the road, you that dwell in Shaphir*: the line is corrupt.
We cannot be sure what its original sense was, but it probably
contained a pun, like most of the others. *have not the people of*

[a] Beth-achzib has: *prob. rdg.; Heb.* The houses of Achzib have.
[b] *Heb.* achzab.

Zaanan gone out...?: here it is the verb 'go out' and the name Zaanan that are similar in Hebrew. *Beth-ezel is a place of lamentation, she can lend you support no longer*: another corrupt line. The N.E.B.'s restoration finds a word-play on *Ezel* and 'support'.

12. *to the very gate of Jerusalem*: Micah seems to be envisaging disaster coming on Jerusalem through an attack from the west. It did in fact sometimes happen that invading armies, even from the direction of Mesopotamia, found it easier to cut through on to the coastal plain. They did this by following the main trade route through the plain of Esdraelon, the lowland area which stretches from the Carmel peninsula through to the Jordan valley, and makes a broad gap in Palestine's highland spine. From the coastal plain they were then able to approach Jerusalem through the low western foothills, and avoid the more difficult terrain to its east and north. An army attacking from this direction would mop up the very villages among which Micah is raising the alarm.

13. *Lachish* was one of the main fortified towns west of Jerusalem, and any army approaching Jerusalem from this direction would be obliged to subdue Lachish first. The word-play here is on the word *steeds* (*rechesh*) and the name Lachish.

14. *Moresheth-gath*, Micah's own home village, is called simply Moresheth in 1: 1. See also note on verse 10 above. *Beth-achzib has disappointed...*: 'disappointment' in Hebrew is *'achzab*. There is a well-known town of 'Achzib on the Phoenician coast (see map 1) but Micah evidently has in mind some smaller place in his own locality.

15. *Mareshah* can be identified with a high degree of probability with a site quite close to Lachish. *and the glory of Israel shall hide in the cave of Adullam*: as David did when he fled from Saul (1 Sam. 22: 1–2). But the text may be corrupt. A fairly easy emendation of it would read, 'And your glory shall perish for ever, O daughter of Israel.'

16. *Shave the hair from your head*: another mourning custom. ✳

THE DISPOSSESSED

Settled Israel was a peasant society. Every man had his small plot of land. In theory the owner of the land was God, and God had ceded to each Israelite family its own estate in perpetuity. In theory land was not allowed to pass outside the family, and if it did, it must be redeemed by a kinsman, or it must revert to its original owner in the sabbatical year or the year of jubilee (see, for example, Lev. 25, though this form of the law is certainly later than Micah's time).

During the monarchy, whatever the theory of the matter, land did in practice pass out of the hands of the small landholders. When peasants fell into serious debt they often had no option but to sell, and the laws of redemption and jubilee were a dead letter. The independent peasant farmers declined in numbers, their holdings were amalgamated into larger estates, and two new classes came into prominence, the wealthy landowners and the insecure landless workers. This process of social change seems to have been going on at a fast pace during the eighth century, and Micah resists it in the name of God. Isaiah, Micah's contemporary, takes the same stand (Isa. 5: 8). Compare the situation which is described in some detail in Neh. 5. The similarities are striking, though three centuries separate Nehemiah and Micah.

2 Shame on those who lie in bed planning evil and
           wicked deeds
       and rise at daybreak to do them,
           knowing that they have the power!
2   They covet land and take it by force;
           if they want a house they seize it;
       they rob a man of his home
           and steal every man's inheritance.

Therefore these are the words of the Lord: 3

  Listen, for this whole brood I am planning disaster,
    whose yoke you cannot shake from your necks
  and walk upright; it shall be your hour of disaster.

    On that day   4
  they shall take up a poem about you
  and raise a lament thrice told,
  saying, 'We are utterly despoiled:
  the land of the Lord's[a] people changes hands.
    How shall a man have power[b]
  to restore our fields, now parcelled out[c]?'
  Therefore there shall be no one to assign to you   5
    any portion by lot in the Lord's assembly.

  How they rant! They may say, 'Do not rant';   6
  but this ranting is all their own,
  these insults are their[d] own invention.

  Can one ask, O house of Jacob,   7
  'Is the Lord's patience truly at an end?
    Are these his deeds?
  Does not good come of the Lord's[e] words?
    He is the upright man's best friend.'
  But you are no[f] people for me,   8
  rising up as my enemy to my[g] face,
  to strip the cloak from him that was safe[h]

[a] the Lord's: *prob. rdg.; Heb.* my.
[b] have power: *prob. rdg.; Heb.* remove from me.
[c] now parcelled out: *prob. rdg.; Heb.* he will parcel out.
[d] *Prob. rdg.; Heb.* his.
[e] the Lord's: *prob. rdg., cp. Sept.; Heb.* my.
[f] But…no: *prob. rdg.; Heb.* But yesterday.
[g] my: *prob. rdg.; Heb. om.*
[h] the cloak…safe: *prob. rdg.; Heb.* mantle, cloak.

and take away the confidence of returning warriors,

9   to drive the women of my people from their pleasant
       homes

and rob the children of my glory for ever.

10 Up and be gone; this is no resting-place for you,

you that to defile yourselves would commit any
       mischief,

mischief however cruel.

11 If anyone had gone about in a spirit of falsehood and lies,
saying, 'I will rant to you of wine and strong drink', his
ranting would be what this people like.

* 1–2. To acquire other men's land is bad enough in itself,
but this is not all. Those who dispossess the peasants use under-
hand means to compass their ends. They *lie in bed planning evil
and wicked deeds and rise at daybreak to do them.* They do not even
bother to preserve the appearance of legality: *they covet land
and take it by force; if they want a house they seize it.* The affair
of Naboth's vineyard (1 Kings 21), though it took place in the
previous century, is a good illustration of the methods available to the unscrupulous rich.

3. Verse 3 is a self-contained oracle of judgement, with its
own introductory formula, but it neatly parallels the accusation of verses 1–2. The land-grabbers 'lie in bed planning',
but unknown to them someone else is making plans too. *For
this whole brood I am planning disaster,* says the Lord.

4–5. The text is corrupt and we cannot with complete confidence restore it, but it seems to be announcing a piece of
poetic justice. Since the rich have allowed the *land of the
LORD's people* to change hands it will indeed change hands.
The conqueror will come and take it.

6. Again there is confusion in the text, but it appears that
the prophet has been dismissed as a 'ranter', and he is flinging
the epithet back at his critics.

7. The wealthy and powerful think they have the defenceless at their mercy. But the poor have an advocate after all, for God is *the upright man's best friend*.

8. In behaving as they do, the oppressors are ranging themselves against God, *rising up as* (his) *enemy. To strip the cloak from* a man was regarded as a serious act. The cloak is an article which cannot even be retained as a pledge (Exod. 22: 26–7). Cp. Amos 2: 8.

9. Micah draws a pathetic picture of the eviction of a peasant family; the women driven *from their pleasant homes*, the children robbed of their expectations, of their title to a share in God's own land, his *glory*.

10. But the prophet, God's bailiff, has an eviction order to present, too. *Up and be gone . . . you that to defile yourselves would commit any mischief, mischief however cruel.*

Verse 11 is a detached fragment, though in content it is connected with 2: 6. There were professional prophets who would go into trances and utter wild and meaningless words, like drunken men. This really *was* ranting, but Micah's contemporaries made no objection to it. Why should they? This kind of prophesying did not give them uncomfortable consciences. This is not to say that serious and respectable prophets did not indulge in ecstatic speech and behaviour. They evidently did. In 2 Kings 3: 15–16 Elisha apparently has to go into a trance before he can prophesy, and needs musical accompaniment to help him to do so. Compare also 1 Sam. 10: 5–6, where Saul finds the ecstatic behaviour of a band of prophets somewhat infectious. On the similarity of religious ecstasy and drunkenness, see Acts 2: 13. ✳

HOPEFUL WORDS

I will assemble you, the whole house of Jacob;   12
  I will gather together those that are left in Israel.
I will herd them like sheep in a fold,
like a grazing flock which stampedes at the sight of a man.

13   So their leader breaks out before them,
        and they all break through the gate and escape,
            and their king goes before them,
            and the LORD leads the way.

* Someone during the period of the exile added these more
optimistic verses to the collection of Micah's oracles. In verse
12 the author is thinking of the divine shepherd gathering
again the flock of Israel, *like sheep in a fold*. But in verse 13 he
changes the metaphor a little. This time the picture in his
mind is not that of the flock being gathered into the safety
of the fold, but of the flock stampeding from the enclosure,
to freedom, the bell-wether at their head. *

THE GUILTY LEADERS

In chapter 3 Micah turns to the leaders of the nation, much as
Hosea does in Hos. chapters 4 and 5, and condemns in turn
the rulers, the prophets and the priests.

3 And I said:

    Listen, you leaders of Jacob, rulers of Israel,
        should you not know what is right?
2   You hate good and love evil,
        you flay men alive and tear the very flesh from their
            bones;
3   you devour the flesh of my people,
        strip off their skin,
            splinter their bones;
        you shred them like flesh[a] into a pot,
            like meat into a cauldron.

[a] like flesh: *so Sept.*; Heb. as.

166

Then they will call to the LORD, and he will give them 4
       no answer;
when that time comes he will hide his face from
       them,
    so wicked are their deeds.

These are the words of the LORD concerning the 5
prophets who lead my people astray, who promise prosperity in return for a morsel of food, who proclaim a
holy war against them if they put nothing into their
mouths:

Therefore night shall bring you no vision,   6
    darkness no divination;
    the sun shall go down on the prophets,
    the day itself shall be black above them.
Seers and diviners alike shall blush for shame;   7
    they shall all put their hands over their mouths,[a]
    because there is no answer from God.

But I am full of strength,[b] of justice and power,   8
    to denounce his crime to Jacob
        and his sin to Israel.
    Listen to this, leaders of Jacob,   9
        rulers of Israel,
    you who make justice hateful
    and wrest it from its straight course,
    building Zion in bloodshed   10
        and Jerusalem in iniquity.
    Her rulers sell justice,   11
    her priests give direction in return for a bribe,

[a] *Lit.* moustaches.
[b] *Prob. rdg.; Heb. adds* the spirit of the LORD.

her prophets take money for their divination,
> and yet men rely on the LORD.
'Is not the LORD among us?' they say;
'then no disaster can befall us.'

12
> Therefore, on your account
Zion shall become a ploughed field,
Jerusalem a heap of ruins,
and the temple hill rough heath.

✻ 1. *And I said* is the introductory formula to the oracle of verses 1–4. The *leaders of Jacob*, the *rulers of Israel*, are the very people who ought to know what is right and uphold it. That is their job. But they are the ones who stand justice on its head, who 'hate good and love evil' (verse 2).

2–3. It is also their job to look after their people. Not only in Israel but elsewhere in the ancient near east rulers were often spoken of as 'shepherds', a metaphor which well illustrates what ideas were held of rulers' responsibilities. But Israel's rulers are interested only in living off the flock, in devouring their flesh, in shredding them *like meat into a cauldron*.

4. They have given no help to God's people, so when they themselves need help it will not be forthcoming. *When that time comes he will hide his face from them.*

5. *These are the words of the LORD:* another introductory formula, showing that the verses which follow were not originally connected with verses 1–4, but have been placed here because of the similarity of subject-matter.

All the canonical prophets had to contend with other members of their own profession who did not join them in their condemnations or their predictions of doom, but continued to *promise prosperity*. Micah is convinced that such prophets only prophesy as they are paid. Whoever feeds them can have their oracles of salvation. The only people they criticize are those who *put nothing into their mouths*.

6–7. Therefore *prophets...seers and diviners alike*, whatever their chosen methods of foretelling the future, will find themselves with nothing to say, *because there is no answer from God.*

8. But Micah himself has plenty left to say. He has not run out of inspiration. This is the proof that he is right and the rest are wrong. When his optimistic opponents are reduced to silence God still gives him strength and power to denounce.

9–11. The general picture of a corrupt society agrees well with that presented by Isaiah for the south and by Amos and Hosea for the north. The specific evil which Micah picks out is the prevalence of bribery. Rulers, priests and prophets are all accused of complicity in this. *Her rulers sell justice, her priests give direction in return for a bribe, her prophets take money for their divination.* Micah also agrees with the other eighth-century prophets when he alleges that the people in general are unaware that their behaviour is an offence against God. Whatever may be said of morality, religion is booming. *And yet men rely on the LORD. 'Is not the LORD among us?' they say; 'then no disaster can befall us.'*

12. Briefly and bluntly Micah sets out the consequences of this corruption. The city and its temple will be destroyed. This prophecy was not in fact fulfilled in the way Micah expected. The only enemy in Micah's time capable of inflicting such destruction was Assyria, and this is no doubt the agent he has in mind. But though the Assyrians overran northern Israel, and it looked for a while as though they would overrun Judah too, they never actually did so. The destruction of Jerusalem did not take place until well over a century later and the invaders were not the Assyrians but the Babylonians. ✳

A remnant restored in an age of peace

We now enter on the second section of the book of Micah (see p. 11). Very little of the material in this section, chapters 4–5, comes from the time of Micah. The real eighth-century prophet was a prophet of doom. This later material is very different indeed in its tone.

THE FUTURE OF ZION

Chapter 4 consists of a number of oracles concerned with Jerusalem's glorious future, perhaps placed here in deliberate contrast with the pessimism of chapter 3 and the disaster predicted in its last verse.

4 1*[a]* In days to come
  the mountain of the LORD's house
  shall be set over all other mountains,
  lifted high above the hills.
  Peoples shall come streaming to it,
2 and many nations shall come and say,
 'Come, let us climb up on to the mountain of the
   LORD,
  to the house of the God of Jacob,
  that he may teach us his ways
  and we may walk in his paths.'
 For instruction issues from Zion,
  and out of Jerusalem comes the word of the LORD;

[a] *Verses 1–3: cp. Isa. 2: 2–4.*

he will be judge between many peoples   3
and arbiter among mighty nations afar.
    They shall beat their swords into mattocks
      and their spears into pruning-knives;
nation shall not lift sword against nation
    nor ever again be trained for war,
    and each man shall dwell under his own vine,   4
      under his own fig-tree, undisturbed.
For the LORD of Hosts himself has spoken.

All peoples may walk, each in the name of his god,   5
but we will walk in the name of the LORD our God
    for ever and ever.

    On that day, says the LORD,   6
      I will gather those who are lost;
I will assemble the exiles and I will strengthen the
      weaklings.
    I will preserve the lost as a remnant   7
    and turn the derelict into a mighty nation.
The LORD shall be their king on Mount Zion
    now and for ever.
And you, rocky bastion, hill of Zion's daughter,   8
    the promises to you shall be fulfilled;
    and your former sovereignty shall come again,
    the dominion of the daughter of Jerusalem.

    Why are you now filled with alarm?   9
      Have you no king?
      Have you no counsellor left,
    that you are seized with writhing like a woman in
      labour?
Lie writhing on the ground like a woman in childbirth, 10

O daughter of Zion;
for now you must leave the city
and camp in the open country;
and so you will come to Babylon.
There you shall be saved,
there the LORD will deliver you from your enemies.

11   But now many nations are massed against you;
they say, 'Let her suffer outrage,
let us gloat over Zion.'

12   But they do not know the LORD's thoughts
nor understand his purpose;
for he has gathered them like sheaves to the threshing-
floor.

13   Start your threshing, daughter of Zion;
for I will make your horns of iron,
your hooves will I make of bronze,
and you shall crush many peoples.
You shall devote their ill-gotten gain to the LORD,
their wealth to the Lord of all the earth.

✷ Verses 1–4 make up a very famous passage. Verses 1–3 are
duplicated almost word for word in Isa. 2: 2–4, and the first
half of verse 4 has affinities with Zech. 3: 10. This duplication
illustrates very clearly one feature of the way prophetic books
were composed. There must have been a considerable number
of 'floating' oracles, not attributed to any particular prophet,
which a compiler could draw on. This rather attractive oracle
has found its way into two separate collections. It was probably
spoken originally by neither Micah nor Isaiah.

The oracle presents a picture of a world in which all nations
acknowledge the lordship of Israel's God, and men from all
over the world make pilgrimages to Jerusalem. The striking
thing is that the prophet does not think of Jerusalem as the

centre of political domination, but of religious enlightenment. What the nations come for, primarily, is teaching, instruction, and to hear *the word of the LORD.*

There is no evidence that anyone conceived of such an idea as early as the eighth century, though Deutero-Isaiah, before the end of the sixth century, seems to have held similar views. Not only is Jerusalem itself not a centre of political domination. The prophet envisages a world in which nobody at all exercises domination, in which war is abolished and warlike weapons and warlike skills are redundant. This is an appealing picture. The prophet gives no hint of how this state of affairs is to be arrived at, though it is evidently to be sustained by the submission of international disputes to divine arbitration; for God *will be judge between many peoples and arbiter among mighty nations afar* (verse 3).

Verse 5 is an astonishing insertion. It is an explicit denial of the prophecy in the preceding four verses. There can be no question, it says, of the Gentiles accepting the God of Israel. *All peoples may walk, each in the name of his god.* The author of this verse appears to be convinced that paganism is perfectly proper for pagans. Israel's God is for Israel alone. In Judaism after the exile there were two schools of thought, the outward-looking, who thought it the job of Jews to offer their faith to the heathen, and the inward-looking, who thought that their duty was to keep the faith to themselves. The conflict between the two schools went on until long after New Testament times.

Verses 6–8 make up another prophecy of Jerusalem's future glory, but one subtly different from that of 4: 1–4. Jerusalem is here thought of not as a centre from which God will instruct a peaceful world, but as the centre of a *mighty nation* (verse 7). The author doubtless has in mind the age of David and Solomon, when Jerusalem's kings ruled a sizeable empire. This is the *former sovereignty* referred to in verse 8. However, what he contemplates is not a mere return to the conditions of the early monarchy. His dreams have no place for an earthly king. He envisages a theocracy. *The LORD shall be their king on Mount Zion now and for ever* (verse 7). Right from the time when the monarchy originated, Israel seems to have been in two minds about it. One party regarded it, at best, as a necessary evil. They were inclined to look back to a golden age before the settlement when Israel had needed no king, and forward to a golden age in which kings would be dispensed with and God reign alone. The other saw the monarchy, in spite of its failures, as God's gift to the nation, and in their picture of the glorious future the Lord's anointed, the messiah, figured prominently.

The most likely date for this oracle is during the exile itself, for verse 6 seems to be thinking of the return from exile as a future possibility.

Verses 9–10 were apparently delivered at a time of impending disaster. If the words *and so you will come to Babylon* are part of the original oracle it would be most appropriately dated a little before 597 or 586 B.C., the occasions when Jerusalem fell to the Babylonians. But there are good reasons for believing that the reference to Babylon is a later gloss. It does not fit into the sense of the passage at all well, for to talk of Babylon as the place where Israel would be saved, and where the Lord would deliver her from her enemies, is very odd. If the line concerning Babylon is removed there is nothing to forbid our attributing the oracle to an eighth-century prophet, and the most natural occasion for its utterance would be towards the very end of the eighth century when Sennacherib and the Assyrians ravaged the country.

In ancient times, when a country was invaded, the country dwellers would flee to the safety of the walled cities. For men to flee in the other direction, from the cities into the country, was a sign of complete hopelessness, an admission that the cities were not secure and that their capture was inevitable. This is the significance of the prophet's advice to *leave the city and camp in the open country; . . . There you shall be saved* (omitting the reference to Babylon). Compare the advice given by Jesus in Mark 13: 14–16 (and parallels). This flight from the city

did take place during the Jewish War of A.D. 66–70, when
people from Jerusalem took refuge in caves in the Dead Sea
area and elsewhere.

Verses 11–13 seem at first sight to be set in a time of war or
threatened war, when *many nations are massed against* Israel.
But this situation is probably not an historical one at all. It
might be eschatological, i.e. the oracle might be looking forward to some great final battle between the Lord's people and
the Lord's enemies, as Ezekiel does in his vision in chapters
38–9 of the battle with Gog and Magog. Or, and this is more
likely, the situation may be a ritual one. One of the themes of
the Autumn Festival was the victory of the Lord's anointed
king over all his enemies, and this is celebrated in a number of
psalms, e.g. Ps. 2 and Ps. 83, which have points of similarity
with the present passage. These verses are probably an oracle
predicting victory and salvation, uttered by a prophet on the
occasion of such a festival. In this connection the harvest
imagery of verse 12 (*for he has gathered them like sheaves to the
threshing-floor*) is significant, for it suggests a harvest festival
setting for the oracle. ✻

ISRAEL'S SAVIOURS

Get you behind your walls, you people of a walled   5:1[a]
    city;[b]

the siege is pressed home against you:[c]

Israel's ruler shall be struck on the cheek with a rod.

But you, Bethlehem in Ephrathah,   2[d]

small as you are to be among Judah's clans,

out of you shall come forth a governor for Israel,

    one whose roots are far back in the past, in days gone
        by.

[a] *4: 14 in Heb.*
[b] Get…city: *prob. rdg., cp.* Sept.; *Heb.* Gash yourself, daughter of
a band.   [c] *So* Sept.; *Heb.* us.   [d] *5: 1 in Heb.*

3   Therefore only so long as a woman is in labour
        shall he give up Israel;
        and then those that survive of his race
        shall rejoin their brethren.
4   He shall appear and be their shepherd
        in the strength of the LORD,
    in the majesty of the name of the LORD his God.
And they shall continue, for now his greatness shall reach
        to the ends of the earth;
5   and he shall be a man of peace.

    When the Assyrian comes into our land,
        when he tramples our castles,
    we will raise against him seven men or eight
        to be shepherds and princes.
6   They shall shepherd Assyria with the sword
        and the land of Nimrod with bare blades;
    they shall deliver us from the Assyrians
        when they come into our land,
            when they trample our frontiers.

* It is possible that verses 1-4 should be taken as part of the preceding oracle in 4: 11-13. If not, there is certainly a connection between the themes of the two passages, and 5: 1-4 is likely to belong to the same festal setting as 4: 11-13.

Verse 1 is very difficult. The Revised Version has, 'Gather thyself in troops, O daughter of troops.' But it is doubtful whether the Hebrew verb concerned really can mean 'to gather in troops'. The N.E.B. has been guided by the Septuagint. The Septuagint has read another verb, spelled slightly differently, and produces the sense: 'You are walled about, O daughter, with a wall.' A third suggestion is: 'You are

176

RSV

cutting yourself severely.' This last would make the verse a reference to the practice of ritual laceration. We know from non-biblical sources that this was widely practised in ancient near eastern religions, and certainly in the religion of the Canaanites. There is a well-known Old Testament reference to it in 1 Kings 18: 28, where the prophets of Baal on Mount Carmel gash themselves with knives. But there is no direct evidence that such laceration was ever used in the worship of Israel's national God. (See also comment on Hos. 7: 14.)

The second half of the verse, *Israel's ruler shall be struck on the cheek with a rod*, does look like a very clear reference to a ritual practice known from Mesopotamian sources, the ritual abasement of the king. In the Akitu Festival, the New Year Festival of the Babylonians, the king was at one stage deprived of his crown and other regalia and struck on the cheek by the priest. After this ritual humiliation he resumed his royal dignity. This verse seems to confirm not only that such rituals were sometimes carried out in Israel, but also that the present passage is part of, or was inspired by, such a ritual.

2–5 a. After such a ritual abasement and restoration it was natural that oracles should be delivered predicting success for the king (this certainly happened in the Babylonian version of the rite). These well-known verses were doubtless in origin such an oracle. They are 'messianic' in the sense that they promise greatness to the Lord's anointed. This oracle is likely to be pre-exilic in date, however, and so the anointed whom the prophet has in mind is more likely to be a contemporary king than any future ideal ruler. He is certainly not thinking of any supernatural figure. The verb rendered by the N.E.B. *shall come forth* could just as readily be understood in the present tense.

2. *Bethlehem in Ephrathah*: Ephrathah (or Ephrath) seems to have been an old name for the region in which Bethlehem was situated. Later copyists of the scriptures, working presumably after the name had gone out of use, misunderstood it as an alternative name for Bethlehem itself. This has caused

confusion in one or two texts, e.g. the story in Gen. 35: 16–20.

3. As it has just been enacted in the ritual drama, so may it be in real life, that defeat and humiliation should be short-lived. This is the meaning of the verse as the N.E.B. has translated it. There is some obscurity in the language of the first half of the verse, which may be due to a scribe who was thinking of Isa. 7: 14 and allowed this to influence what he wrote. The second half of the verse, *and then those that survive of his race shall rejoin their brethren*, was almost certainly added to the original pre-exilic oracle by someone who lived during the exile itself. The words attempt to make the oracle more relevant to the exilic situation. They look forward to the return of the exiles to their homeland and give the whole oracle a future reference.

4. *He shall appear:* the Hebrew is literally, 'and he shall stand'. The N.E.B.'s translation no doubt accurately reflects the later understanding of the words, when they were taken to refer to a future king who would lead the restored Israel. *and be their shepherd:* on the application of the title 'shepherd' to rulers see the comment on 3: 2–3.

5. *and he shall be a man of peace:* the existing verse division of the Hebrew text attaches this clause to what follows, probably wrongly, as the N.E.B. translation suggests. If we do connect the words with what follows it is necessary to translate differently: 'And this shall be peace....'.

Verses 5 b–6 form a separate oracle, predicting Israel's rescue from the Assyrians by several *shepherds and princes*. This is likely to be an eighth-century oracle, and may well be by Micah himself. Assyria was not a military threat to Israel after the beginning of the seventh century. Some scholars suggest, however, that the oracle is a late one after all, and that the name 'Assyria' was conventionally used in later times for Israel's current enemies, almost as a kind of code name. Compare the way the book of Revelation uses the name 'Babylon' as a cipher for 'Rome', as it does, e.g., in chapter 18.

6. *The land of Nimrod* here means Assyria, though the legendary hero and king, Nimrod (see Gen. 10: 8–9), is in our surviving texts associated with Babylon rather than Assyria. *

THE REMNANT VICTORIOUS AND THE
REMNANT PURIFIED

All that are left of Jacob, surrounded by many peoples, 7
    shall be like dew from the LORD,
    like copious showers on the grass,
    which do not wait for man's command
    or linger for any man's bidding.
All that are left of Jacob among the nations, 8
    surrounded by many peoples,
shall be like a lion among the beasts of the forest,
    like a young lion loose in a flock of sheep;
as he prowls he will trample and tear them,
    with no rescuer in sight.
Your hand shall be raised high over your foes, 9
and all who hate you shall be destroyed.

On that day, says the LORD, 10
I will destroy all your horses among you
    and make away with your chariots.
I will destroy the cities of your land 11
    and raze your fortresses.
I will destroy all your sorcerers, 12
and there shall be no more soothsayers among
    you.
I will destroy your images and all the sacred pillars in 13
    your land;
you shall no longer bow in reverence before things
    your own hands made.

179

14   I will pull down the sacred poles in your land,
         and demolish your blood-spattered altars.
15   In anger and fury will I take vengeance
         on all nations who disobey me.

* Here we have two oracles relating to the future of Israel. The first, verses 7-9, looks forward to a time when Israel will take vengeance on her enemies and reign supreme in the earth. *Your hand shall be raised high over your foes, and all who hate you shall be destroyed* (verse 9). Two metaphors lead up to this climax. The second is comprehensible enough. Israel is described as a lion at large in the forest, or among *a flock of sheep* (verse 8). But the metaphor of verse 7 is at first sight odd. Israel *shall be like dew from the LORD, like copious showers on the grass*. Dew and showers are normally used in the Old Testament as images of beneficence, but to see such a significance in them here would be out of character with the rest of the passage. There is, however, an instructive use of the same simile in 2 Sam. 17: 12, where Hushai contemplates how Absalom's rebel army may overcome David. They will 'descend on him like dew falling on the ground, and not a man of his family or of his followers will be left alive'. The point of the simile here is that the dew is silent, irresistible and thorough. Something similar seems to be in the prophet's mind in the present instance. The dew and showers *do not wait for man's command or linger for any man's bidding*. No human power can control them. So will be the forces of God's resurgent people.

The oracle of verses 10-15 looks forward very differently, to the purification of Israel by the removal of the false objects of her trust. These include her armed forces, her *horses* and her *chariots* (verse 10); her fortifications, her *cities* and *fortresses* (verse 11); her superstitions, her *sorcerers* and *soothsayers* (verse 12); her corrupt religion, her *images* and *sacred pillars* (verse 13), *sacred poles* and *altars* (verse 14). The eighth-century prophet Isaiah condemns both dependence on idols and dependence on horses and chariots; and, like the present oracle, he condemns both in the same breath. See, e.g., Isa. 2: 7–8. The same prophet also condemns superstition and necromancy (Isa. 8: 19–20). It is clear, therefore, that there is nothing in the present oracle that could not have been uttered by an eighth-century Judaean prophet.

13. *sacred pillars:* see note on Hos. 3: 4.

14. *sacred poles:* see note on Hos. 4: 12.

15. *In anger and fury will I take vengeance on all nations who disobey me:* up to this point the oracle has been predicting divine judgement on Israel. This verse can hardly have belonged to it originally (if the text is correct). It has been added by an editor or scribe who could not resist the thought that if God so punished his own people for disobedience he must surely punish more severely the unrepentant heathen. Alternatively, we might emend the word 'nations' to 'the proud' (reading *gewim* for *goyim*). ✱

Israel denounced for her people's sins

GOD'S CASE AGAINST ISRAEL

Chapter 6 is mostly in the form of a lawsuit, in which God, as both accuser and judge, indicts and then pronounces sentence on his people. Into this passage has been inserted verses 6–8, a famous oracle which is, however, on quite a different subject.

Hear now what the LORD is saying: 6

Up, state your case to the mountains;
let the hills hear your plea.
Hear the LORD's case, you mountains,   2

you everlasting pillars that bear up the earth;
for the LORD has a case against his people,
    and will argue it with Israel.

3   O my people, what have I done to you?
    Tell me how I have wearied you; answer me this.

4   I brought you up from Egypt,
        I ransomed you from the land of slavery,
    I sent Moses and Aaron and Miriam to lead you.

5   Remember, my people,
    what Balak king of Moab schemed against you,
and how Balaam son of Beor answered him;
    consider the journey*a* from Shittim to Gilgal,
        in order that you may know the triumph of the
        LORD.

6   What shall I bring when I approach the LORD?
    How shall I stoop before God on high?
Am I to approach him with whole-offerings or yearling
        calves?

7   Will the LORD accept thousands of rams
        or ten thousand rivers of oil?
    Shall I offer my eldest son for my own wrongdoing,
        my children for my own sin?

God*b* has told you what is good;
    and what is it that the LORD asks of you?
    Only to act justly, to love loyalty,
    to walk wisely before your God.

Hark, the LORD, the fear of whose*c* name brings success,
    the LORD calls to the city.

[a] consider the journey: *prob. rdg.; Heb. om.*
[b] God: *prob. rdg.; Heb. obscure.*   [c] *So Sept.; Heb.* thy.

Listen, O tribe of Judah and citizens in assembly,[a]   10
can I overlook[b] the infamous false measure,[c]
    the accursed short bushel[d]?
Can I connive at false scales or a bag of light weights? 11
    Your rich men are steeped in violence,   12
        your townsmen are all liars,
    and their tongues frame deceit.
    But now I will inflict a signal punishment on you   13
        to lay you waste for your sins:
    you shall eat but not be satisfied,   14
        your food shall lie heavy on your stomach;
        you shall come to labour but not bring forth,
        and even if you bear a child
        I will give it to the sword;
    you shall sow but not reap,   15
you shall press the olives but not use the oil,
    you shall tread the grapes but not drink the wine.
    You have[e] kept the precepts of Omri;   16
        what the house of Ahab did, you have done;
        you have followed all their ways.
    So I will lay you utterly waste;
        the nations[f] shall jeer at your citizens,
        and their insults you shall bear.

* 1–2. The advocate in an Israelite court customarily began
by appealing to mountains and hills, earth and heaven, to God
himself and to the assembled multitude to bear witness to the
truth of what he was saying. Now *the LORD has a case against*

[a] citizens in assembly: *prob. rdg.; Heb. unintelligible.*
[b] can I overlook: *prob. rdg.; Heb. obscure.*
[c] *Prob. rdg.; Heb. adds* infamous treasures.
[d] *Heb.* ephah.   [e] You have: *so Sept.; Heb.* He has.
[f] the nations: *so Sept.; Heb.* my people.

his people, and the prophet, his advocate, speaking on his behalf, begins in accepted fashion by stating his *case to the mountains* and to *the hills* and to the *everlasting pillars that bear up the earth*. The earth is pictured as supported by these pillars above the abyss of waters.

3–5. Speaking now God's own words in the first person, the prophet moves into phase two of the argument. God has kept his part of his contract with Israel. He has done everything he could for them; brought them *up from Egypt*; ransomed them *from the land of slavery*. He gave them leaders, *Moses and Aaron and Miriam*, and enabled them to overcome the enemies they met on the way to the promised land, such as *Balak king of Moab* (see Num. 22–4). *Shittim* was the last staging post in the wilderness and *Gilgal* the first encampment in the promised land. Between the two was the unpleasant episode described in Num. 25, in which the Israelites were seduced into the worship of the Baal of Peor and were horribly punished by a plague; the sending out of the spies into Canaan and their promising reception in Jericho by Rahab (Josh. 2); and finally the miraculous crossing of the Jordan itself (Josh. 4). *the triumph of the LORD:* the word translated 'triumph' is literally 'righteousnesses' or 'righteous acts'. But the word 'righteousness' in Hebrew has a very interesting range of meanings. It not infrequently bears the meaning which it undoubtedly carries here, 'vindication', 'victory'.

Verses 6–8 break into the speech for the prosecution. They make up an independent oracle on the subject of sacrifice and its usefulness. Israelite religion before the settlement in Canaan seems to have made only modest use of sacrifice. The elaboration of the institution took place in Palestine, doubtless under Canaanite influence, and there were always those in Israel who resisted the development. This strand of opinion, which placed a low value on sacrifice, if it did not reject it altogether, existed at least as early as Amos (see Amos 5: 25) and perhaps earlier (cp., for example, 1 Sam. 15: 22). In the eighth century, Hosea (see 6: 6 and 8: 13) and Isaiah (Isa. 1: 12–13) appear to share the same reservations about sacrifice, and in the follow-ing century Jeremiah rejects it quite emphatically (7: 21–3). As late as New Testament times there were rabbis who did not regard sacrifice highly, and who interpreted the command to offer it as one of God's purely arbitrary injunctions.

Once it is conceded that sacrifice is an appropriate way to worship God, where does one draw the line? *Am I to approach him with whole-offerings or yearling calves?*: the whole-offering was the most lavish sacrifice of all, for every scrap of it was burnt on the altar, the worshipper eating none at all. But is this enough? If the God of the whole earth is to be rightly worshipped will not *thousands of rams* be needed, and (the prophet takes off into hyperbole) *ten thousand rivers of oil?* Oil was mixed with the cereal offering and was also an acceptable sacrifice in itself. If sacrifice is appropriate at all, how can one stop short of the most precious sacrifice, the sacrifice of one's children? The prophet's argument is thus a *reductio ad absurdum*. If this is the conclusion to which logic takes us then our pre-mise, that God requires sacrifice, must have been wrong at the start.

Shall I offer my eldest son for my own wrongdoing, my children for my own sin? This is often interpreted as implying that human sacrifice was practised at the time when these words were uttered. The correct conclusion to be drawn is exactly the reverse. The question is a rhetorical one. *Shall I offer my eldest son...?* Of course not! No one would consider such a thing. Everyone knows how horrified God would be at such an offering. Well then, argues the prophet, do the ordinary sacrifices of rams, calves or oil really make any better sense? It is true that there are sporadic references to human sacrifice in the Old Testament. In 2 Kings 16: 3 it is said that king Ahaz (735–715 B.C.) 'even passed his son through the fire'. In 2 Kings 21: 6 the same is said of Manasseh (687–642 B.C.). If these accusations are justified the acts were certainly the result of assimilation to heathen ways of worship. At no time was there any question that human sacrifice was a legitimate part of the worship of Israel's national God (cp. Jer. 7: 31).

8. It is possible that this verse is a separate statement, originally unconnected with the foregoing, but the connection with the preceding verses is a very natural one and it is perhaps best taken as part and parcel of the whole oracle. If sacrifice is not what God requires, what is man's duty to God? *To act justly, to love loyalty, to walk wisely before your God* is an important summary statement of one variety of Israelite piety. It has often been called the high-water mark of Old Testament religion, but it would be more accurate to call it the high-water mark of Old Testament moralism. On the word *loyalty* see the note on Hos. 2: 19. The Hebrew word translated *to walk wisely* is a rare one and we cannot be absolutely certain of its meaning. Older translators favoured 'humbly'.

Is the oracle of verses 6–8 by Micah himself? There is nothing in the sentiments expressed which could not have been uttered in the eighth century, but the manner of their expression, especially in verse 8, seems to owe more to the post-exilic wisdom writers than to the pre-exilic prophets.

In verses 9–10*a* the speech for the prosecution is resumed, with an appeal this time, not to the mountains and hills but to the populace, the *tribe of Judah and citizens in assembly*. Israelite legal proceedings were normally held in the city gate, i.e. in the most public place possible, and all passers by were called to bear witness to them.

10*b*–12. When he comes to the substance of the charges against the nation the prophet is surprisingly brief. They are exactly the kind of offences condemned a few years earlier by Amos in the north: the *false measure*, the *short bushel*, the *false scales* and *bag of light weights*. Compare Amos 8: 4–6, and see the comments thereon.

In verses 13–16 the prophet passes from accusation to sentence, the counsel for the prosecution becomes judge. That one person should fulfil both roles would be an affront to our sense of justice, but in Israel impartiality, in this sense, was not held to be a virtue, and there was nothing to prevent a judge turning advocate, or vice versa.

14–15. The curses here are similar in tone to those of Amos 5: 11, on which see the comment.

16. *You have kept the precepts of Omri; what the house of Ahab did, you have done:* Omri, and Ahab his son, were by any objective criteria outstandingly strong rulers, but to the writers of the Old Testament they were outstanding only in wickedness. They were northern kings and their mention here suggests the possibility that this whole judgement speech was originally uttered against the Northern Kingdom. If this last supposition is correct the judgement speech must be dated in the eighth century and may well be by Micah himself. There is nothing in it which could not belong to the eighth century and much that reflects the conditions of that time. ✳

Disappointment turned to hope

Chapter 7 is a collection of miscellaneous oracles. There is a clear break in the chapter after verse 13, but the structure of the first thirteen verses is extremely problematical. The passage has insufficient unity of theme to be treated as a single poem, but no unanimity has been reached as to how it should be analysed into separate ones.

THE NATION IN TURMOIL

Alas! I am now like the last gatherings of summer **7**
    fruit,
      the last gleanings of the vintage,
      when there are no grapes left to eat,
    none of those early figs that I love.
    Loyal men have vanished from the earth,   2

there is not one upright man.
All lie in wait to do murder,
each man drives his own kinsman like a hunter into the
    net.

3   They are bent eagerly on wrongdoing,
    the officer who presents the requests,[a]
    the judge who gives judgement[b] for reward,
    and the nobleman who harps on his desires.

4   Thus their goodness is twisted[c] like rank weeds
    and their honesty like briars.[d]
    As soon as thine eye sees, thy punishment falls;
    at that moment bewilderment seizes them.

5   Trust no neighbour, put no confidence in your closest
        friend;
    seal your lips even from the wife of your bosom.

6   For son maligns father,
    daughter rebels against mother,
        daughter-in-law against mother-in-law,
        and a man's enemies are his own household.

✶ Verse 1 begins in the style of a lament. *Alas! I am now like
the last gatherings of summer fruit, the last gleanings of the vintage:*
it is the stale, flat time which follows the last of the harvests
(the harvest of grapes and olives) and its great festival. The
time when salvation and renewal were annually expected has
come and gone. We are reminded of the words of Jeremiah
(8: 20), 'Harvest is past, summer is over, and we are not
saved.'

2–3. But immediately, in typical prophetic fashion, the

[a] the requests: *prob. rdg.; Heb. om.*
[b] who gives judgement: *prob. rdg.; Heb. om.*
[c] twisted: *prob. rdg.; Heb. obscure.*
[d] their honesty like briars: *prob. rdg.; Heb. obscure.*

author breaks off lament and turns to castigation. The reason for his depression is the corrupt state of society. There are some obscurities in the description but the main lines are clear enough. The corruption is total. *Loyal men have vanished... there is not one upright man.*

4. There follows, in very brief form, the promise of punishment. *As soon as thine eye sees, thy punishment falls; at that moment bewilderment seizes them*: this might naturally be taken as the climax of the poem, and some critics do indeed see it as ending at this point.

In verses 5–6 we revert, however, to the subject of the low moral state of society, though in somewhat different terms. This is an anticlimax after verse 4, but not very good as a prelude to verse 7 and what follows.

5–6. A society in which a man can *trust no neighbour*, and *put no confidence in* his *closest friend* or his *wife*; a society in which families are divided *and a man's enemies are his own household*, is one in the throes of dissolution. We cannot guess, however, when the words might have been uttered. They could be applicable to any seriously troubled time. ✳

PIOUS HOPE

But I will look for the LORD,   7
I will wait for God my saviour; my God will hear me.
   O my enemies, do not exult over me;   8
      I have fallen, but shall rise again;
though I dwell in darkness, the LORD is my light.
I will bear the anger of the LORD, for I have sinned 9
      against him,
until he takes up my cause and gives judgement for me,
until he brings me out into light, and I see his justice.
Then may my enemies see and be abashed,   10
those who said to me, 'Where is he, the LORD your God?'

> Then shall they be trampled like mud in the streets;
>   I shall gloat over them;

11   that will be a day for rebuilding your walls,
>   a day when your frontiers will be extended,

12   a day when men will come seeking you
>   from Assyria to*a* Egypt
>   and from Egypt to the Euphrates,
>   from every sea and every mountain;*b*

13   and the earth with its inhabitants shall be waste.
>   This shall be the fruit of their deeds.

* Verses 7–10 are very much in the style of a psalm. If they are intended to follow on verses 5–6 in sense they would naturally be taken as expressing the author's grief at the state of affairs just described. In this case they suggest that the author himself has suffered much from the hatred of his fellows. But they read more appropriately if attached to verses 11–13. We should then take them as words put into the mouth of the nation, Israel, and see their setting as the exile.

One possible solution to the problem of the division of the passage is to attach verse 7, alone, to what precedes. The author would then be contemplating the dissolution of society but resting his hope in God. *But I will look for the LORD, I will wait for God my saviour.* If this expedient be adopted then it is verse 8 which makes a new beginning.

Whether the unit should be 7–13 or 8–13 the words of this section express sentiments which would be very natural to the nation in exile. In verse 8, she has *fallen, but shall rise again.* She dwells *in darkness*, i.e. in foreign captivity. In verse 9 she acknowledges that the exile is the just result of her own faults. *I will bear the anger of the LORD, for I have sinned against him.* But she looks forward to vengeance on her enemies (verse 10).

[a] to: *so one MS.; others* cities.
[b] from every...mountain: *prob. rdg., cp. Sept.; Heb.* sea from sea and mountain of the mountain.

Verse 11, prophesying the rebuilding of the walls, also follows very naturally. Israel in exile was led to hope not only for restoration but for dominion. She looks for a day when her *frontiers will be extended*; when her dominion will run *from Assyria to Egypt.* ✳

ISRAEL AVENGED

Shepherd thy people with thy crook,   14
    the flock that is thy very own,
that dwells by itself on the heath and in the meadows;
let them graze in Bashan and Gilead, as in days gone by.
Show us[a] miracles as in the days when thou camest out 15
    of Egypt;
let the nations see and be taken aback for all their might, 16
    let them keep their mouths shut,
        make their ears deaf,
    let them lick the dust like snakes,   17
        like creatures that crawl upon the ground.
Let them come trembling and fearful from their
        strongholds,
    let them fear thee, O LORD our God.

✳ Verses 14-17 make up another post-exilic or exilic poem on a similar theme.

14. *Shepherd thy people with thy crook*: the translation 'crook' takes a small liberty. Palestinian shepherds did not use crooks. The Hebrew word signifies something more like a club. *Bashan* and *Gilead* are areas which were famous for their good pastures and their cattle.

17. *let them lick the dust like snakes*: that snakes eat dust was erroneously believed by the Israelites. Cp. Gen. 3: 14. ✳

[a] *Prob. rdg.; Heb.* I will show him.

THE FORGIVING GOD

18 Who is a god like thee? Thou takest away guilt,
     thou passest over the sin of the remnant of thy own
          people,
          thou dost not let thy anger rage for ever
          but delightest in love that will not change.

19   Once more thou wilt show us tender affection
               and wash out our guilt,
          casting all our[a] sins into the depths of the sea.

20   Thou wilt show good faith to Jacob,
          unchanging love to Abraham,
     as thou didst swear to our fathers in days gone by.

✶ 18–20. *Who is a god like thee?*: this type of statement about
God's incomparability may in its form be a survival from poly-
theistic ways of thinking, but it should not necessarily be
assumed that an Israelite who used this form would have
conceded the existence of other gods.

The remnant: the idea of the remnant is an extremely important one, for it helped to solve, in so far as it could be
solved at all, the prophets' theological dilemma of how to
reconcile the absolute righteousness and the everlasting love of
God. God could judge his people, and destroy them, but
nevertheless save enough of them (the remnant), penitent,
purified, to serve as the nucleus of a renewed Israel. Thus is
his righteousness vindicated but his purposes of salvation do
not fail. This idea came into prominence with Isaiah, though
it already existed in earlier Israelite traditions, e.g. the story
of Noah, and the story of the career of Joseph. Our present
passage has nothing to say about the universality of God's
mercy and forgiveness. It is for *the remnant of thy own people*.
His *good faith* is shown *to Jacob*, and his *unchanging love to
Abraham*, i.e. to his chosen people.

[a] *So Sept.; Heb.* their.

The *love that will not change* is the *ḥesed* on which comments were made at Hos. 2: 19. Elsewhere the word is translated by the N.E.B. as 'loyalty'.

Some critics regard verses 18–20 as part of the same poem as 14–17. Whether they were originally connected or not we should probably see them as emanating from the same background, viz. the exilic or post-exilic period. Though the pre-exilic prophets and their condemnations went almost unheeded, the fall of Jerusalem to the Babylonians seemed to vindicate them. They were therefore taken seriously in retrospect. Once the exile had happened, it was generally conceded that the prophets had been right after all, and most Israelites were then ready enough to see the disaster as a punishment for sin, and to acknowledge the need for repentance and forgiveness. Verses 18–20 are a product of this mood. Unlike the poems earlier in this chapter they do not look forward merely to a reversal of the nation's fortunes. They accept that forgiveness comes first, and they declare confidently that it will be forthcoming, because God is a forgiving God.

Thus in this passage which is considerably later than the eighth century we see something of the achievement of the eighth-century prophets. Amos is far more convinced of God's firmness and justice than he is of God's readiness to forgive. Hosea, equally convinced with Amos that the God of righteousness cannot overlook sin, wrestles with the problem of how the God of love can in the last resort utterly abandon his own. When the words of the present passage were uttered the judgement which Amos regarded as so irrevocable had fallen. The repentance for which Hosea had so insistently and unsuccessfully appealed during his lifetime had been forthcoming. And the character of God as one who will assuredly punish the sinner and as assuredly forgive the penitent is securely grasped. *

*   *   *   *   *   *   *   *   *   *   *   *   *

A NOTE ON FURTHER READING

Readers requiring fuller and more detailed treatment of Amos and Hosea might consult the commentaries by J. L. Mays in the *Old Testament Library* series (S.C.M., 1969), and that of R. S. Cripps, *A Critical and Exegetical Commentary on the Book of Amos* (S.P.C.K., 1955).

Brief but valuable commentaries are those in the *Torch* series (S.C.M.) by J. Marsh on Amos and Micah (in one volume) and by G. A. F. Knight on Hosea. One-volume commentaries may also usefully be consulted, especially the 'New Peake's Commentary'. (Longmans, 2nd ed. 1967.)

For background material readers are referred to articles in the bible dictionaries, to *The Living World of the Old Testament*, by B. W. Anderson, and to the relevant volumes of *The New Clarendon Bible* (Oxford University Press), by G. W. Anderson on *The History and Religion of Israel* (1966), and by E. W. Heaton on *The Hebrew Kingdoms* (1968). The *Sourcebook for Teachers*, edited by R. C. Walton (S.C.M., 1970), may also be included here.

INDEX

Abraham 12, 80, 92
Achan 86
Achor 86
Achzib (in Judah) 158, 160, 161
Achzib (in Phoenicia) ix, 161
Acts of God 24, 32, 95
Adulterous wife, prosecution of 83
Ahab 1, 14, 17, 30, 78, 183, 187
Ahaz x, 4, 73, 105, 155, 185
Akitu festival 177
Altar 21, 29, 30, 64, 101, 123, 131, 132f., 137, 180
Amaziah 2, 9, 53, 56, 57, 58, 59
Ammon, Ammonites xi, 17, 19
Amorites 21
Anath 71
Animal gods 107
Appearance of God, see Theophany
Aram (Syria) ix, x, 15f., 19, 52, 67, 102, 105, 107, 145f.
Ark 129
Ashdod ix, 15, 28, 29, 158
Asherah 100; see also Sacred pole
Ashimah 63
Ashkelon ix, 15, 158
Assyria 1f., 16, 29, 31, 32, 47, 49, 57, 105, 106, 107, 112, 113, 116, 117, 119, 122, 123, 124, 125f., 127, 132, 133, 137f., 140f., 151f., 169, 174, 178, 179, 190, 191
Authority, prophetic 8, 26, 58f.
Autumn festival 14, 45, 60, 65, 90, 100, 113, 125, 145, 175, 188
Aven, see Beth-aven
Aven, vale of 15f.
'awen 144
Azariah, see Uzziah
Baal 33, 65, 71ff., 82, 84, 85, 86f., 88, 110, 118, 132, 136, 177
Baalism, baal-worship 72f., 84, 88, 96, 103, 109, 125, 130, 131, 132, 137, 146
Baal-peor 103, 128f., 184
Babylon 18, 117, 169, 172, 174, 177, 178, 179, 193

Baker 114f.
Balaam 14, 59, 182
Bashan 31, 32, 191
Beersheba ix, 39, 40, 63, 64
Ben-hadad 15, 16
Benjamin 105f.
Beth-aven 99, 101, 105, 106, 132
Beth-eden 15f.
Bethel ix, 2, 9, 29, 30, 32, 33, 39, 45, 56, 57, 63, 101, 106, 112, 121, 135, 142
Beth-ezel 158, 159, 161
Beth-le-aphrah 158f.
Bethlehem ix, 158, 175, 177
Betrothal 87f.
Boundary stones 106
Bow 117f.
Bozrah ix, 17
Bribery 43, 169
Bull images 63, 120f., 145; see also Calf-god
Calf-god 120f., 132, 147; see also Bull images
Call, of prophets, 8, 53, 58f.
Canaanite mythology 71, 104, 150; pantheon 71; worship and religion 71ff., 90, 91, 100, 110, 177
Canaanites 71ff., 85, 124, 144, 150
Caphtor 67
Carmel ix, 12, 64, 66, 118, 161, 177
Catchword 10
Conquest of Canaan 84
Court (of justice) 41, 42, 83, 138
Covenant 5, 6, 22, 23, 26, 27, 36, 43, 73, 79, 90, 87, 90, 95f., 111, 118, 119, 120, 124, 129, 131, 133, 145
Crete 67
Cult 33, 40, 46, 47, 83
Cultic forms of speech 24
Curse 7, 14, 59, 70, 130
Cushites 67
Damascus ix, 14f., 16, 45, 47
Dan ix, 63, 121
David 68, 70, 80, 89, 92f., 160, 161, 173, 180

195

INDEX

Jezebel 17

Jezreel ix, 75, 78, 79, 80, 81, 87

Joel 45

Joshua 80

Josiah 92

Jotham x, 4, 73, 155

Judah ix, 1f., 18, 40, 56, 59, 64, 70, 105f., 107, 146, 155, 156, 157, 169, 183; mentioned in Amos 12, 20, 56; mentioned in Hosea 73, 75, 79, 99, 101, 103, 104, 106, 110, 111, 112, 124, 140f., 142

Judgement, divine 22, 26, 30, 37, 46, 53, 57, 60, 65, 69, 85, 98, 128, 133; prophetic 36

Judgement sayings 42

Justice, just 23, 33, 41, 42, 43, 44, 51, 108, 109, 133, 134f., 139, 143, 167, 168, 182, 189, 192, 193

Karnaim ix, 52

King, as divinely appointed 6, 91

King, Israelite 54, 57, 89, 92f., 102, 114f., 119f., 122, 131, 133, 135, 166, 171, 173f., 178; see also Monarchy

King, non-Israelite 132f., 137, 150, 177

Kingship of God 139

Kir 15f., 67

Knowledge of God 88, 94, 95, 104, 108, 109, 110, 119, 120

Laban 145, 146

Lachish ix, 158, 159, 161

Lament, lamentation 38f., 44, 46, 62, 118, 188f.

Law 20, 119f., 123

Lebanon 16, 52, 151, 153

Leviathan 66

Lion 25, 26, 27, 29, 30, 44, 46, 106, 130, 140, 148, 179, 180

Lo-ammi 75, 79, 80, 87

Locust 53f.

Lord, as divine title 13

Lo-ruhamah 75, 79, 80, 87

Love 73, 75, 136f., 139, 152, 154, 192

Manasseh, king x, 185

Manasseh, tribe 102

Mareshah 158, 160, 161

Marriage of Hosea 3, 9, 74ff., 80ff., 85, 89f.

Menahem x, 107, 122

Mesha, king of Moab 19

Mesopotamia 117, 161

Messiah 177

Micaiah 65

Milkom 19

Mizpah 102f.

Moab ix, 18, 19, 182, 184

Moabite Stone 19

Monarchy 78, 80, 90, 91, 92f., 97, 114, 120, 128, 141, 148f., 162, 173f., see also King

Moresheth 155, 160, 161

Moses 182, 184

Moth, god of death 71, 84, 150

Mourning 45, 62, 63

Naboth 78, 164

Nazirite 21, 24

New Moon 61, 82, 84

New Year Festival 115, 177

Nomad 12f., 31, 67

Obadiah 19

Omri 30, 183, 187

'On 144f.

Oral tradition 7

Oral transmission 7, 8, 9, 10

Oven 114f.

Passover 47

Patriarchs 47, 144, 147

Pekah x, 133

Pekahiah x

Penitence 45, 109, 151, 152

Pentateuch 47, 141

Persia 117

Philistines, Philistia x, 15, 16, 48, 67

Pilgrim feast 44, 46, 62, 126

'Place symbolism' in Hosea 78, 80, 86

Plague 35, 51, 53, 84, 110, 150

Pledge 21, 23

Plumb-line 55

Polytheism 192

Poor 21, 23, 41, 61

Priest, priesthood 56, 59, 91, 93, 94, 95, 96, 97, 98, 100, 102, 111, 112, 132, 133, 137, 138, 166, 167, 169

Priestly formula 40

Prophetic symbolism 76–8

Prophets 21, 24, 25, 58, 96, 127, 145, 165, 166, 168, 169

197